Pub
Superchefs

recipes from Britain's best pub kitchens

Pub Superchefs
Editor: Susan Nowak

Cover design: McKie Associates
Photography: Tracey Sherwood
Home Economist: Veronica Miller
Illustrations: McKie Associates

Managing Editor: Mark Webb

Printed by Interprint, Malta

ISBN 1-85249-162-0

Published by CAMRA Books, Campaign for Real Ale
Ltd, 230 Hatfield Road, St Albans AL1 4LW

© CAMRA Books 2000

CONTENTS

Foreword by Matthew Fort, Food Editor of the Guardian   8
Introduction   … … … … … … … … … … … … … … … …9
Author's Notes   … … … … … … … … … … … … … … …10

SOUPS AND STARTERS   … … … … … … … … … … …11
Lettuce And Coriander Soup   … … … … … … … … … …12
Potato And Fresh Herb Soup   … … … … … … … … … …13
Nettle Soup   … … … … … … … … … … … … … … … …14
Barszcz (Beetroot Soup)   … … … … … … … … … …15
Soup A La Reine   … … … … … … … … … … … … … …16
Camembert And Broccoli Soup   … … … … … … … … …17
Stilton Soup … … … … … … … … … … … … … … … …18
Pat's Fresh Fish And Shellfish Soup   … … … … … …19
Haggis Consommé   … … … … … … … … … … … … …20
Hot Avocado With Stilton Sauce   … … … … … … … …21
Little Jack Horner … … … … … … … … … … … … … …22
Potted Silloth Shrimps   … … … … … … … … … … … …23
Devilled Crab   … … … … … … … … … … … … … … …24
Creebridge Smokey Ramekins   … … … … … … … …25
Fish Terrine With Herb Sauce   … … … … … … … … …26
Potted Duck … … … … … … … … … … … … … … … …27

FISH   … … … … … … … … … … … … … … … … …29
Supreme Of Halibut With A Crab, Coriander And Cous-Cous
Crust On Herb Scented Leeks With Red Pepper Coulis   …30
Monkfish With Horseradish And Chervil Sauce   … … …31
Sautéed Monkfish … … … … … … … … … … … … … …32
Salmon And Crab Cakes With Fresh Spicy Tomato Sauce 33
Filo Cases Of Sander In Muscadet Sauce … … … … … …34
Fresh Salmon Bake   … … … … … … … … … … … … …35
Linguini With Mascarpone And Smoked Salmon   … … …36
Salmon Fusilli   … … … … … … … … … … … … … … …37
Salmon En Croûte   … … … … … … … … … … … … …38
Lobster Mcphee   … … … … … … … … … … … … … …39
Pillows Of Crab   … … … … … … … … … … … … … …40
Creamy Fish Pie   … … … … … … … … … … … … … …41
Baked Plaice With Seafood Stuffing   … … … … … … …42
Quick Fried Squid With Chillies And Garlic … … … … …43

MEAT, POULTRY AND GAME 45

Lamb In Orange And Rosemary Gravy 46
Lamb Pie 47
Lava Lamb (In Pastry Case) 48
Honey And Mustard Glazed Lamb 49
Lample Pie 50
Dalesman's Pie 51
Baked Lamb With Rosemary 52
Braised Beef In Honey And Ginger 53
Steak Cameron 54
Evesham Pie 55
The Butterleigh Inn Burger 56
Suckling Pig Roasted With Honey And Ginger 57
Somerset Pork, Honey And Wholegrain Mustard Hot Pot 58
White Horse Somerset Pork 59
Pork Escalope In Pernod 60
Pork Escalope In A Caramelised Apple Sauce 61
Humble Pie 62
Pork Conor 63
Burton House Pig's Fry 64
Bacon Pudding 65
Rhineland Pie 66
Alison's Alston Pie 67
Sausage Pie And Pickles 68
Farmbridge Pie 69
Huntingdon Fidget Pie 70
Supreme Of Chicken With A Salad Of Marinated Peppers 71
Oldbury Chicken 72
Chicken Supreme In Sherry 73
Roman Hazelnut Chicken 74
Chicken Apricot 75
Barbary Duck Oak Style 76
Roquefort And Venison Crumble 77
Jugged Yorkshire Hare 78
Casserole Of Local Game 79
Rabbit Pie With Lemon And Herbs 80
Northumbria Rabbit Casserole 81
Haytor Rabbit Casserole 82
Pigeon And Black Cherry Casserole 83
Wood Pigeon Gateaux With Prune Mayonnaise 84

VEGETARIAN 85
Yvonne's Bread Pudding 86
Crispy Filo Parcel Of Wild Rice And Leeks With A Cherry
Tomato And Wine Sauce 87
Lavabread, Leek And Caerphilly Cheese Rissoles 88
Ricotta And Pea Pie 89
Red Pepper And Gruyère Tart 90
Vegetable Crumble 91
Crostini Of Mushrooms And Basil 92
Cheesy Leek And Potato Bake 93
Garlic Potatoes 94
Winter Warmer Potatoes 95
Spicy Red Cabbage 96
Vegetarian Mushroom Creole 97
Mushrooms A La Grecque 98
Courgette, Mushroom And Tomato Sauce 99
Grenadine Onions 100

ETHNIC 101
Hokkien Braised Pork 102
Malay Chicken Curry 103
Thai Pork Tenderloin 104
Stuffed Chicken Breasts Thai Style 105
Indonesian Fish Hotpot 106
Sri Lankan Fish Curry 107
Beef Embul 108
Sri Lankan Omelette 109
Siam Chicken 110
Nepalese Chicken Korma 111
Aloo Dum 112
Vegetable Curry 113
Masoor Dal With Slices Of Potatoes And Nuts 114
Masala Chops 115
Keema Curry 116
Spiced Lamb With Water Chestnuts 117
Cotes De Porc A L'ardennaise 118
Californian Rabbit Casserole 119
Pollo Cacciatora 120

SNACKS/SAUCES/PICKLES 121

Mad Dog Clanger 122
Oxfordshire Bacon Clanger 123
The Driftwood Spars Cornish Pasty 124
Scotch Eggs 125
Cullen Skink 126
Goathland Broth 127
Blue Cheese Tartlets 128
Stovies 129
Rift Valley Chicken Livers 130
Bacon, Mushroom And Cheese Filled Jackets 131
Three Elms Club Sandwich 132
Bolognese Flan 133
Mexican Burritos 134
Peach, Onion And Red Pepper Relish 135
Apple Chutney 136
Bay Horse Apricot And Apple Chutney 137
Tangy Barbecue Sauce 138

PUDDINGS 139

Steamed Marmalade Castles 140
Lily's Ecclefechan Tart 141
Old English Treacle Tart 142
Chocolate Bread And Butter Pudding 143
Spicy Hostry Bread Pudding 144
Bread And Butter Pudding 145
Apple Charlotte Maltese Style 146
Hot Oat And Banana Slice 147
Glazed Strawberries In Horseradish And Black Pepper
Sabayon 148
Individual Victorian Trifle With Strawberries 149
Negroni Alla Panna 150
Orange And Brandy Syllabub 151
White Chocolate And Bailey's Mousse 152
Summer Fruit Surprise 153
Caramelised Tart Lemon Tart 154
Dixie Bourbon Pie 155

BEER RECIPES **157**
Cheese And Ale Soup 158
Broccoli And Stilton Soup 159
Welsh Rarebit With Abbot Ale 160
Ale Fondue 161
Wings Of Skate 162
Cod In Beer Batter 163
Fisherman's Pie 164
Wellington Greene 165
Belhaven Rabbit 166
Lamb Pie With Apricots And Old Speckled Hen 167
Braised Beef With Murphy's And Kumquats 168
Steak And Stilton Pie 169
Venison Collops With Cranberries And Shallots Served With
Deep Fried Celeriac 170
Highgate Steak Pudding 171
Braised Beef With Brown Ale And Wild Mushrooms ...172
Home-Made Sausages 173
Haggis, Potato And Turnip Fritters Served With A Real Ale
And Onion Gravy 174
Pumpkin, Apple And Beer Chutney 175
Beer Cheese 176
Beer Tart 177

CIDER RECIPES **179**
Rabbit With Cider And Coriander 180
Sausage Casserole 181
Porc Mynwy Cylchian And Gig Porc Mewn Ddwr And Sats
A Winwns 182
Stuffed Turnips Baked In Cider 183
Cider Pie 184

FOREWORD

Pubs are the future of eating out in this country. Food writers and restaurant critics may be dazzled by the great culinary melting pot of London, but for most of us it is in pubs up and down the country (and even in London) where some of the most interesting and plain, downright delicious cooking is now to be found. Increasingly the best and brightest of our chefs are opting for the more accessible, informal, and, let's face it, fun environment to show off their skills, sourcing their raw materials from the locality, and bringing pride in our own culinary traditions where before there was hardly any. With this splendid collection of recipes, of course, we can now cook all these terrific dishes at home. Which means our pub chefs will have to come up with new recipes to keep us coming back for more.

Matthew Fort, Food Editor, The Guardian newspaper

INTRODUCTION

In 1989 when I edited the first Good Pub Food guide for the Campaign for Real Ale, pub chefs were sneered at as providers of pub grub. How times have changed. Many are now winning awards for their innovative cooking, and the term 'gastro pub' was born.

When I invited chefs to send me their best recipes for inclusion in the first guide, I had no idea what I was unleashing.

Would I get any at all? Chefs, as we know, can be prima donnas and many of them guard their recipes jealously.

But not pub chefs, as it turned out. Not only is this splendid breed almost totally devoid of the pretensions which afflict so many of their restaurant colleagues, they are generous souls who like to talk about their cooking and share their recipes. A decade later in 1999 when I edited the fifth Good Pub Food I had so many recipes to include that, for the first time, the guide had a recipe index. This prompted me to look through all five guides and I discovered that over the years pub cooks had sent getting on for 200 recipes.

They ranged through all styles from traditional to modern, regional to ethnic, and covered every course of a meal from soups and starters through meat, fish and vegetarian to some wonderful puds.

So I decided to bring them all together in a recipe book, and here it is. I have always believed it is people who make pubs, and there is a great range of real characters among the chefs who contributed the recipes in this collection. Many of them I have met and talked to, and reading their recipes brings back warm memories of chatting about food over a pint of real ale.

Creative chefs are now choosing to make pubs rather than restaurants their platform, bringing us great food in an informal pub atmosphere where we can drink beer as well as wine.

Increasingly they are interested in beer cuisine - there is a whole chapter of beer recipes in this book - and in partnering beer with food, chalking up beer lists with tasting notes. It all adds up to a real buzz in the kitchens of our best pubs - and I'm sure that as you use their recipes you'll get a taste of their enthusiasm as well. Cheers!

AUTHOR'S NOTES

This is a cookery book, not a guide book. The recipes were collected over a period of 10 years and are attributed to the pubs and chefs who sent them originally. Some of them have moved on by now - some who were employed by publicans might have their own pubs - or may have retired. Sadly, some of the pubs themselves have closed. So while enjoying the recipes please don't assume that they will still be on the menus of the pubs concerned, or that the same chef will be cooking there.

Because the recipes have been sent in separately by different chefs, there are a number of discrepancies in the translation between imperial and metric measurements. We have maintained the original interpretations because these most closely represent what the chef intended in the recipe.

SOUPS AND STARTERS

LETTUCE AND CORIANDER SOUP

A light and lovely soup from Libby Casson at the Red Cow, Nantwich in Cheshire. Makes a great soup to start with.

INGREDIENTS
(SERVES SIX)

1 large iceberg lettuce, roughly chopped

1 tspn freshly ground black pepper

3 bunches lightly chopped spring onions

600 ml (1 pint) milk

100 g (4 oz) fresh coriander

75 g (3 oz) butter

2 cloves garlic, crushed

600 ml (1 pint) vegetable stock

METHOD

Melt the butter and briefly fry the spring onions; add garlic, coriander and black pepper, then the lettuce and 600 ml (a pint) of boiling vegetable stock. Simmer for 5 minutes, put through the blender, and add the milk. Reheat gently without boiling "as the soup shouldn't lose its lovely, crunchy texture."

POTATO AND FRESH HERB SOUP

From the Free Press in Cambridge comes a delicious but simple soup, using inexpensive ingredients. "Perfect for a cold winter's day," says cook Karen Billows.

INGREDIENTS
(SERVES SIX)

50 g (2 oz) butter

100 g (4 oz) onions – diced

425 g (15 oz) potatoes – peeled and diced

1 tspn salt, freshly ground pepper

2-3 tspns in total of parsley, thyme, lemon balm and chives – finely chopped

1.2 litres (2 pints) chicken stock (or cube)

130 ml (4 fl oz) creamy milk

METHOD

Melt the butter in a heavy saucepan. Add the potatoes and onions, and toss until well coated with butter. Season, cover and sweat gently for 10 minutes. Add fresh herbs and stock. Cook until the vegetables are soft then purée or liquidise. Adjust seasoning and thin with the milk to required consistency. Serve sprinkled with chopped herbs.

NETTLE SOUP

From the Hillside Bar at Hillsborough, Northern Ireland, former local CAMRA Pub of the Year, comes a 'free' soup of nettles.

INGREDIENTS

2 large bunches of nettles (wear gloves to pick!)
1 large onion
1-2 leeks
50 g (2 oz) margarine
50 g (2 oz) flour
1½ litres (2 pints) chicken stock
Bouquet garni
Salt and pepper
A little sour cream
Chopped parsley

METHOD

Sweat off chopped onion and leeks in margarine, and stir in flour. Cook for 2 minutes on low heat, add rinsed chopped nettles, stock and seasoning. Next add bouquet garni and simmer for 30 minutes, then remove bouquet garni and put through blender or sieve. Correct seasoning and add a little sour cream. Top with chopped parsley.

BARSZCZ (BEETROOT SOUP)

My husband (of Polish origin) and I spent a happy afternoon at the Pot of Beer in Manchester, while the rain bucketed down outside, talking about Poland to owner Wanda, also with Polish ancestry, and Peter Ward, who gave me this smashing recipe.

INGREDIENTS

1.25 kg (2½ lb) fresh raw beetroot
5 stock cubes
1 tblspn cider vinegar
2 tblspns brown sugar
4 tblspns red wine
Cream to serve
50 g (2 oz) butter
Half an onion
2 heaped tblspns plain flour
Grating of black pepper
1 tspn dill
For vegetable stock:
1 leek
1 onion
1 carrot
1 parsnip
1 bay leaf
½ tspn peppercorns

METHOD

Leaving skins on, wash beetroot thoroughly, place in cold water, bring to the boil and simmer until tender, approximately 1-1½ hours. Peel beetroot (easier when still warm) and grate coarsely. Chop vegetables coarsely, place all ingredients in cold water, bring to the boil and simmer for 45 minutes. To slightly thicken soup, melt butter and fry onion gently until soft and slightly golden, add flour, then some water and add to simmering stock. Strain stock, bring liquid up to 3.4 litres (6 pints), add stock cubes, cider vinegar, brown sugar and wine. Bring to the boil. Add grated beetroot, freshly ground pepper and dill. Warm through gently and turn off heat. (If cooked for too long beetroots lose their colour.)

SOUP A LA REINE

A warming soup from Philippa and Bob Bone at the Marquis of Lorne, a 16th Century mellow stone inn at Nettlecombe, Dorset.

INGREDIENTS

150 g (6 oz) butter
2 onions, roughly chopped
2 large parsnips, peeled and roughly diced
50 g (2 oz) plain flour
2 cloves garlic
2 tspns curry powder
300 ml (½ pint) cream
Seasoning to taste
2 litres (4 pints) chicken stock
Chopped parsley

METHOD

Fry parsnips, onions and garlic in the butter until lightly browned. Add flour and curry powder and cook for 1 minute, stirring. Add stock and seasoning and simmer for 30 minutes. Put through a blender. Stir in cream and serve hot with croutons and a little fresh-chopped parsley sprinkled on top.

CAMEMBERT AND BROCCOLI SOUP

A popular soup, bursting with flavour, from the Steps House, Stourport-on-Severn, Worcs.

INGREDIENTS

50 g (2 oz) butter
2 medium onions, chopped
500 g (1 lb) broccoli florets
600 ml (1 pint) chicken stock
2 tspns cornflour
125 ml (¼ pint) milk
500 g (1 lb) Camembert, cubed – use less if you don't want too strong a taste

METHOD

Fry onion gently in butter until soft. Add broccoli, fry for 5 minutes, stirring, then add stock. Simmer until tender, add milk mixed with cornflour, and simmer until thickened, then add cheese and purée in blender. Reheat gently.

STILTON SOUP

Chef/landlord Eric Welek comes up with some innovative dishes at the Tudor Oaks on the A1 northbound at Astwick on the Herts/Beds border, but this soup is more traditional.

INGREDIENTS
(SERVES FOUR)

1 medium onion, finely chopped

25 g (1 oz) flour

300 ml (½ pint) milk

450 ml (¾ pint) chicken stock

175 g (6 oz) Stilton, finely diced

Salt and pepper to taste

4 tblspns double cream

Croutons to garnish

METHOD

Heat butter in pan with onions, cook gently for several minutes, until soft but not browned. Blend in flour and gradually add milk and stock. Bring to boil, stir, simmer for 10 minutes when thickened. Add cheese, seasoning and cream. Stir over low heat until cheese is nearly melted. Top with croutons when serving.

PAT'S FRESH FISH AND SHELLFISH SOUP

At the White Hart in the village of Sherington near Newport Pagnell, Bucks, landlady Pat Aisthorpe is joint cook. Here is her recipe for a hearty fish soup that's almost a stew – she makes a large quantity which would be ideal if you had a dozen or so round, or halve the quantities.

INGREDIENTS (SERVES 15)

1.2 litres (2 pints) cider

3 fish stock cubes

3 tomatoes (chopped)

1 large onion (chopped)

3 courgettes (chopped)

3 large fillets smoked haddock

2 tuna steaks

2 swordfish steaks

24 mussels

Cornflour

Garlic butter

Plenty of fresh chopped parsley

METHOD

Gently fry chopped onions in garlic butter until soft. Add chopped courgettes and cider. Simmer to reduce for 10 minutes then add tomatoes. Poach the fish, removing any bones and dice, then add to the pan with some of the stock and the fish stock cubes. Add the mussels (after cleaning) and cook on a low heat for 20 minutes while the mussels open. Before serving, add a little cornflour to thicken. Serve in a pre-heated bowl, topped with fresh parsley and crusty bread.

HAGGIS CONSOMME

Chef, Martin Mitchell, made the Johnson House at Balerno near Edinburgh famous for using traditional ingredients in unusual ways.

INGREDIENTS
(SERVES FOUR)

600 ml (1 pint) each of clear mutton stock and clear veal stock

20 Won Ton crackers

500 g (1 lb) haggis

4 tblspns whisky

Beaten egg to glaze

Little flour

METHOD

Reduce the two pints of stock to around 1 pint by fast simmering, and keep hot. Shape 20 dumplings from the haggis. Wrap each in a Won Ton wrapper, sealing with egg wash and flour, then poach in the stock. Arrange five cooked dumplings in a deep soup plate, adding 1 tblspn of whisky. Pour stock over each serving.

HOT AVOCADO WITH STILTON SAUCE

This quick and easy starter is a good way to use up over-ripe avocados, says Susan Richardson, award-winning chef at the Star Inn, Weaverthorpe, North Yorks.

INGREDIENTS
(SERVES TWO)

1 avocado pear
75g (3 oz) cubed Stilton
150-175 g (4-6 oz) béchamel sauce
2 tblspns double cream

METHOD

Cut avocado in half and remove stone. Skin, slice and fan out both halves, dividing between two dishes. Gently heat the béchamel, add cheese and heat gently until melted; then stir in cream and simmer gently until thickened. Pour over the avocado then heat under a hot grill for 2 or 3 minutes.

LITTLE JACK HORNER

From the Gordon Arms Hotel in Kincardine O'Neil comes a simple but effective starter using soft ewe's milk cheese. They call it 'Little Jack Horner'.

INGREDIENTS
(FOR EACH PORTION)

50 g (2 oz) soft ewe's cheese

Fresh bread crumbs

Oil for frying

Shredded lettuce

Sliced tomato and cucumber

25 g (1 oz) each plum and apricot conserve

METHOD

form the soft ewe's milk cheese into a croquette (they use St Finan Broomhill as it keeps its shape well and is made with vegetable rennet), and coat with fresh breadcrumbs. Fry gently in oil for 1-2 minutes each side. Place on shredded lettuce with tomato and cucumber. Melt 25 g (1 oz) each of plum and apricot conserve and pour over.

POTTED SILLOTH SHRIMPS

Produce used at the Pheasant Inn, Bassenthwaite Lake in Cumbria comes from the surrounding area – damsons, rhubarb and herbs from the kitchen garden, smoked Cumberland ham from Wabberthwaite, smoked venison, duck and lamb, and game from the woods and fields. Here Silloth shrimps from the local fishmonger are transformed into a starter full of tasty morsels.

INGREDIENTS

450 g (1 lb) peeled shrimps

175 g (6 oz) unsalted butter

Pinches of salt, cayenne, nutmeg and mace

Garnish:

Lemon wedges

Buttered wholemeal bread

Shredded lettuce

METHOD

Melt butter gently, do not allow to brown; add shrimps and turn until they are all well coated in butter then season to taste with the salt and spices. Divide into small pots, press down with a light weight, leave to set in the fridge and turn out to serve garnished with lemon wedges, wholemeal bread and butter, and shredded lettuce.

DEVILLED CRAB

Crab is best, in my view, simply boiled and served cold. But I enjoyed this starter, which would make a good opening to a dinner party, from the Anchor Inn, Oldbury-on-Severn.

INGREDIENTS
(SERVES SIX AS A STARTER)

1 small onion, skinned and chopped

1 tspn Worcester sauce

75 g (3 oz) breadcrumbs

100 ml (8 fl oz) double cream

2 tspns English mustard

450 g (1 lb) crab meat (dark and white mixed)

1 tspn salt

15 g (½ oz) butter

Few drops Tabasco

Grated cheese and breadcrumbs

METHOD

Saute chopped onion in butter until transparent; mix in salt, mustard, Tabasco, Worcester sauce and crab meat. Add the cream and mix well, then finally stir in the breadcrumbs, making sure they are well moistened. Rest in the fridge for an hour. Divide into six ovenproof dishes, top with breadcrumbs/grated Cheddar and bake in medium oven (180°C, 350°F, gas mark 4) for around 35 minutes until bubbling and browned on top. Serve with a side salad.

CREEBRIDGE SMOKEY RAMEKINS

From the Creebridge House Hotel at Newton Stewart, Dumfries and Galloway, a starter using smoked salmon and haddock:

INGREDIENTS (MAKES 12 POTS)

250 g (8 oz) smoked salmon
175 g (6 oz) smoked haddock
125 g (4 oz) butter
1/2 onion, chopped
2 tblspns plain flour
Salt and black pepper
600 ml (1 pint) cream
175 g (6 oz) Cheddar
1 tspn English mustard
300 ml (1/2 pint) fish stock
Breadcrumbs

METHOD

Saute chopped onion in a frying pan until brown, add smoked salmon and haddock and cook for 2-3 minutes, add a tablespoon of plain flour and mix in with the juices and butter until they are soaked up, adding a little more flour if necessary. Pour in fish stock slowly, stirring all the time, until the mixture thickens, then add grated Cheddar off the heat, allowing the cheese to melt; season, add mustard and cream, stir well and return to gentle heat until cheese has fully dissolved. Pour into ramekins, top with breadcrumbs, brown under grill and serve.

FISH TERRINE WITH HERB SAUCE

The King's Arms in Old Amersham, Bucks, has a good mention in the Michelin guide. Here is their recipe for a sophisticated starter.

INGREDIENTS

2 large lemon soles

500 g (1 lb) whiting

3 egg whites

3 slices bread soaked in milk

210 ml (7 fl oz) double cream

1 soupspoon tomato purée

1 tspn nutmeg

1 soupspoon chopped chives

1 tspn chopped dill

175 g (7 oz) chopped onions

175 g (7 oz) sliced mushrooms

50 g (2 oz) butter

4 large pancakes

Salt and pepper to taste

METHOD

Skin and fillet the soles and whiting; gently fry the onion and mushrooms in the butter. Blend the whiting to a purée in a food processor and season with salt, pepper, nutmeg, chives, dill, and tomato purée. Add the squeezed-out bread and blend well. Blend in the egg whites and chill for an hour. Add the cold cream. Oil a rectangular terrine and line it with the pancakes. Mix a quarter of the fish purée with the mushroom mixture. Spread half the remaining purée over the base of the terrine and cover with the seasoned sole fillets. Next spread a layer of the fish and mushroom mixture. Finish with a layer of fish purée. Fold over the flaps of pancake to cover, lay a sheet of buttered foil on top and bake in a bain marie or tin one-third filled with water in a moderate oven (180°C, 350°F, gas mark 4) for about 1½ hours.

POTTED DUCK

And here is another clever recipe from The Kings Arms in Old Amersham, Bucks offered us by their chef Gary Munday.

INGREDIENTS (SERVES 12)

1 large Aylesbury duck, roasted, flesh removed and chopped into small dice

2 small onions, diced

1 tspn ground ginger

1 tspn Chinese five spice

5 juniper berries

3 cloves

3 bay leaves

Juice and zest of 1 orange

1 glass port

1 clove garlic

1 tspn chopped tarragon

600 ml (1 pint) duck stock made from carcass

Ground black pepper

1 small bunch chopped parsley

25 g (1 oz) aspic powder

METHOD

Sweat off the onions in a large saucepan and add all the ingredients except the parsley and aspic. Simmer gently for approx 2 hours until the liquid has reduced. Add the aspic and parsley and spoon the mixture into a terrine mould or ramekins and chill in the refrigerator. Delicious served with a little salad and crusty bread.

GOOD PUB FOOD

Hundreds of pubs feature in this nationwide guide to the best
pub food. Maps and full location descriptions take you to the
door of real ale restaurants which are sure to delight.

The pubs in this book serve food as original and exciting as
anything available in far more expensive restaurants. And, as
well as the exotic and unusual, you will find landlords and
landladies serving simple, nourishing pub fare such as a
genuine ploughman's lunch or a steak and kidney pudding.
Award-winning food and beer writer Susan Nowak, who has
travelled the country to complete this fifth edition of the
guide, says that 'eating out' started in British inns and taverns
and this guide is a contribution to an appreciation of all that
is best in British food...and real cask conditioned ale.

Good Pub Food 5th edition
by Susan Nowak
448 pages approx   Price: £9.99   Use the following code
to order this book from your bookshop: ISBN 1-85249-151-5

FISH

SUPREME OF HALIBUT WITH A CRAB, CORIANDER AND COUS-COUS CRUST ON HERB SCENTED LEEKS WITH RED PEPPER COULIS

Award winning chef Alan Reid creates a great table at the Wheatsheaf, Swinton, in the Scottish Borders. This dish won the first Taste of Scotland and Scottish Seafood competition in 1998.

INGREDIENTS
(SERVES FOUR)

4 x 180-200 g (6-7 oz) fillets of halibut – skin on
100 g (4 oz) white crab meat
2 springs of coriander
100 g (4 oz) cous cous
2 whole leeks
2 sprigs basil
2 sprigs fennel
2 red peppers
100 ml (4 fl oz) olive oil
Seasoning

METHOD

Roast the red peppers, rest in a plastic bag for 30 minutes, then remove skins. Puree with the olive oil and season. Set aside. Add equal amount of boiling water to cous-cous and leave to double in size and cool. Clean and slice the leeks into small dice and sweat off with herbs and seasoning in a little olive oil for 2 minutes, to retain the bright green colour. Sear halibut fillets in hot olive oil, skin side down. Lightly season. Turn over and place in a hot oven for 4–5 minutes. Mix crab, cous-cous and chopped coriander in a bowl. Place the fish on a clean tray, remove skin and top with cous-cous mixture. Place under the grill until golden brown. Place fish in the centre of the hot plate on top of the sautéed leeks. Drizzle the warmed pepper coulis around, and garnish with fresh herbs.

MONKFISH WITH HORSERADISH AND CHERVIL SAUCE

The Anchor Inn at the aptly named "Beer in Devon" is strong on fish. Here is a simple but effective supper dish.

INGREDIENTS (FOR ONE GENEROUS PORTION):

250 g (8 oz) trimmed monkfish tail

125 ml (4 fl oz) double cream

2 tspns coarse horseradish sauce

1 tspn chopped fresh chervil

1 sprig chervil

2 tspns lemon juice

2 tblspns dry white wine

50 g (2 oz) melted butter

METHOD

Cut monkfish into thin slices and place on a buttered grill pan tray. Brush with melted butter and place under moderate grill until lightly browned and cooked through – a few minutes only. Meanwhile put white wine and lemon juice into a saucepan and bring to the boil; remove from heat and add horseradish and cream. Return to lower heat, stirring, and reduce to required consistency; add chopped chervil and season then stir in melted butter from fish. Place fish on a hot plate and pour sauce around and a little over it. Garnish with a sprig of chervil and serve.

SAUTÉED MONKFISH

Patrick Ferguson, chef/landlord at the Three Horseshoes in Powerstock, Dorset, says fish is his "thing", bought from local boats and fish markets. This simple recipe for sautéed monkfish is one of his favourites.

INGREDIENTS
(PER PERSON)

150 g (6 oz) monkfish fillet

1 tspn salt

1 tspn white pepper

1 tblspn ground cumin

100 g (4 oz) plain flour

Unsalted butter

METHOD

Take one 150 g (6 oz) monkfish fillet per person, sliced on the bias to produce a flat escalope around ¼" thick. Mix the salt and white pepper and ground cumin with the plain flour. Toss the escalopes in the seasoned flour and sauté in unsalted butter. Serve with lemon wedges, green salad and French bread.

SALMON AND CRAB CAKES WITH FRESH SPICY TOMATO SAUCE

Kevin Cadman, bronze medallist in the British Open Culinary Championships and chef at the Five Horseshoes, Maidensgrove, near Henley-on-Thames, sent a recipe for one of my very favourite treats.

INGREDIENTS
(SERVES SIX)

450 g (1 lb) potatoes

Salt and pepper

2 tblspns fresh chopped dill and parsley

Juice of half a lemon

225 g (8 oz) flaked poached salmon

100 g (4 oz) white crabmeat

100 g (4 oz) dark crabmeat

Plain flour

1 egg, beaten

Fresh breadcrumbs

3 shallots, chopped

2 cloves garlic, crushed

A little butter

450 g (1 lb) fresh, chopped tomatoes

Splash of wine vinegar

METHOD

Cut potatoes into chunks and boil till cooked, then purée and add salt and pepper to taste, fresh herbs, the juice of half a lemon; fold in flaked poached salmon and white and dark crabmeat. Mix well and allow to cool slightly. Take mixture and roll into tangerine-size balls, then dip in flour, egg and breadcrumbs. Allow to rest and cool. Prior to cooking, flatten into required shape, then deep fry in oil until golden brown and hot in middle. For the tomato sauce: sweat shallots and garlic in a little butter, add fresh chopped tomatoes and a splash of wine vinegar, simmer until soft then blend and sieve. Reduce further and season to taste.

FILO CASES OF SANDER IN MUSCADET SAUCE

From the adventurous menu of the Riverside Inn at Aymestrey in Herefordshire comes a recipe from the Loire.

INGREDIENTS
(SERVES FOUR)

400 g (14 oz) celery, cut into thin strips

500 g (1 lb 2 oz) Sander (or substitute), cleaned, filleted and cut into thin slices as you would smoked salmon

16 sheets filo pastry (this recipe makes 8 parcels)

Sunflower oil for cooking
Salt

Ingredients for the Beurre Blanc:

4 shallots

12 cl Muscadet

350 g (12 oz) unsalted butter, very cold

Salt and pepper

METHOD

Make the beurre blanc by sweating the shallots in a frying pan with the wine. Cook on a low heat until the liquid has been reduced to a thick sauce, add the butter cut into small cubes, and beat together over a low heat until smooth. Remove from the heat, season with salt and pepper, and keep warm.

Preheat oven to 200 C, 400 F, gas 6. Heat a little oil in a pan and fry the celery until soft and brown then drain on kitchen paper and shake a little salt over the strips. Using the same oil, adding more if necessary, fry the fish slices very quickly on both sides. When almost cooked, and just beginning to brown, remove from the pan. Lightly oil a sheet of filo pastry and place a second sheet directly on top. Lay a few slices of the fish, topped with a dessert spoonful of the celery, on one half. Oil the edges and fold over the other half of the square. Seal the edges by turning in and pressing lightly to form an envelope; repeat until you have made all 8 parcels. Make two small slits in the top of each parcel with a sharp knife. Place the parcels on a baking tray and cook in the oven for 10-15 minutes until golden brown and crisp. Serve on a hot plate surrounded by beurre blanc with new potatoes and baby vegetables.

FRESH SALMON BAKE

Excellent fresh salmon is regularly on the menu at the Crown and Trumpet in Broadway, Worcs. Here is a delicious way to serve it hot.

INGREDIENTS (SERVES SIX)

1.25 kg (2½ lb) salmon tail
175 ml (6 fl oz) white wine
3 tblspns fresh chopped dill
50 g (2 oz) breadcrumbs
50 g (2 oz) melted butter
50 g (2 oz) grated cheese
Salt and pepper
475 ml (16 fl oz) double cream
300 ml (10 fl oz) fish stock

METHOD

Place the salmon in an ovenproof dish with the white wine and fish stock and bake for about 45 minutes at 160°C, 325°F, gas mark 3, basting from time to time, until the salmon is cooked. Pour the liquid into a pan; add the cream; season and cook until the sauce thickens. Pour the sauce over the salmon after removing its skin. Mix the breadcrumbs, cheese, dill and butter together, sprinkle over the salmon and grill for 3 to 5 minutes until the top is brown. Serve with new potatoes and a salad garnish.

LINGUINI WITH MASCARPONE AND SMOKED SALMON

Mike Maguire at the Trengilly Wartha threw up his city job to own a pub and fast gained a wide reputation for both bar and restaurant food at the Trengilly near Falmouth in Cornwall. Here is his fast and decidedly decadent recipe.

INGREDIENTS

450 g (1 lb) or more fresh linguini (depending on appetite)

8 tblspns Mascarpone cheese

100 g (4 oz) unsalted butter

225 g (8 oz) smoked salmon scraps cut into 2" slithers

Black pepper

3 litres (approx. 5 pints) boiling, slightly salted water

METHOD

Melt the butter over a gentle heat, add Mascarpone and stir until it all melts. Cook linguini rapidly for a couple of minutes until al dente and drain. Pour sauce into a warm bowl, add smoked salmon strips and a liberal amount of black pepper. Toss in the pasta, using a little cooking water if sauce is too thick. Mix together gently and serve immediately with a green salad and olive bread.

SALMON FUSILLI

Some really delicious meals have been created at the Crown Inn, Wells-Next-The-Sea in Norfolk, by chef Raymond Newell and landlady Jeanette Fenerton. Try this simple pasta dish for starters.

INGREDIENTS

15 g (½ oz) butter
1 shallot (diced)
4 mushrooms (sliced)
1 pinch of dill (fresh if possible)
100-150 g (4-5 oz) diced boned skinned salmon
A splash of white wine
A splash of double cream
150 ml (¼ pint) béchamel (white sauce)
50 g (2 oz) fusilli boiled in salted water until al dente

METHOD

Saute shallot in butter, add mushrooms and salmon then stir gently for 1 minute. Add dill and wine. Simmer for a further minute, add cream and béchamel. Bring to bubbling point and stir in cooked fusilli; serve with fresh bread.

SALMON EN CROUTE

The Black Lion in Lion Street, Hay-on-Wye, Herefordshire, gives a new twist to an old favourite by flavouring salmon en croûte with ginger.

INGREDIENTS
(SERVES FOUR)

1 kg (2 lbs) puff pastry

4 x 175 g (6 oz) salmon supremes (steaks)

50 g (2 oz) fresh peeled ginger

100 g (4 oz) butter

Chopped parsley

Beaten egg to glaze

METHOD

Make ginger butter by finely chopping ginger and a little parsley then blending them with the butter. Roll out puff pastry and cut into eight squares. Place each salmon steak in the centre of a piece of pastry. Divide the ginger butter into four and place a knob on top of each steak, then cover with the other piece of pastry, sealing with egg wash. Score the top, brush with egg wash then bake in a pre-heated oven at 200°C, 400°F, gas mark 6 for around 20 minutes until the pastry is risen and golden, but the fish not overcooked.

LOBSTER MCPHEE

I think this is the first time a recipe has ever been created specifically for the guide. So I thank Archie Davidson, chef at the seafood bar of the Harviestoun Brewery Tap at Strathallan Hotel, Dollar, in Scotland, for this opulent recipe named after his fresh fish supplier.

INGREDIENTS

2 cooked lobsters
Cheese sauce
50 g (2 oz) butter
300 ml (½ pint) milk
5 tblspns Drambuie or Glayva
25 g (1 oz) flour
150 ml (5 fl oz) double cream
1 small onion stuck with a few cloves
Salt and black pepper
1 bay leaf
25 g (1 oz) Dunlop cheese (similar to Scottish Cheddar)

METHOD

Split lobsters in half lengthwise with a sharp knife and remove both halves of stomach sack at top of its head and discard. Also remove and discard blackish intestinal vein which runs through lobster. Scoop out and sieve the brain (soft green/black part) into a small bowl. Remove meat from tail, claws, clawjoints, chest sections and legs. Pull off and discard gills which are attached to the outside of the chest at the leg joints. Scrape away any white matter on inside of shells and add to brain. Cut meat into ½" pieces. Clean shells and put on serving dish in a warm place. Make cheese sauce by simmering onion and bay leaf in milk for 15 minutes; strain and gradually add to a roux made from the flour and butter; season and simmer slowly to thicken, stirring all the time; whisk in grated cheese then stir in sieved brain mixture and check seasoning. Melt butter in large pan; add lobster meat and toss for a few minutes. Sprinkle on liqueur and flame. When burnt out add cheese sauce and cook for a few minutes; add cream and heat. Pour into warmed shells and garnish with chopped parsley.

PILLOWS OF CRAB

In Devon, where there is always plenty of fresh seafood, the chef at the Culm Valley Inn near Cullompton created this delicious starter or light supper dish using crab.

INGREDIENTS
(SERVES TWO)

1 small dressed crab

3 tomatoes, peeled and chopped

1 shallot, finely chopped

Salt and pepper to season

250 g (8 oz) puff pastry

1 tspn fresh chopped basil

1 yellow pepper

120 ml (4 fl oz) tomato juice

50 g (2 oz) butter

METHOD

Roll out puff pastry thinly, and cut into two rounds. Grease a baking tray, place puff pastry on it and cover with greaseproof paper. Cook in hot oven (230°C, 450°F, gas mark 8) for 8-10 minutes. Remove crab from shell and sweat in a little butter with the shallot; season. For the sauce, finely chop yellow pepper and, keeping back a little for garnish, put into small saucepan with tomato juice, basil and tomatoes then reduce a little by simmering fast, and season. Cut puff pastry circles in half, cover one half with crab, top with the other half and brush with melted butter. Pour sauce onto two plates, and put crab pillows on top, sprinkling yellow peppers around the sides.

CREAMY FISH PIE

Doreen Scott's food at The Bell in Odell, Beds, is quite outstanding and I thank her for this lovely recipe for Creamy Fish Pie which she has reduced to a quantity for four-five people.

INGREDIENTS

450 g (1 lb) white fish fillets (Doreen uses cod or coley)

100 g (4 oz) fresh or frozen whole green beans

100 g (4 oz) courgettes

600 ml (1 pint) milk

65 g (2½ oz) butter (plus butter to cook courgettes)

50 g (2 oz) plain flour

½ tblspn horseradish sauce

½ tblspn Worcester sauce

1 tblspn lemon juice

Salt and pepper

Creamed potato

METHOD

Skin fish and cut into 1" cubes; cut cooked beans into ½" lengths; sweat peeled and sliced courgettes in butter until cooked. Melt the butter in a large saucepan, gradually add flour, mix and cook gently for a few minutes; gradually add the milk and mix to a smooth sauce. Remove from the heat and add the horseradish sauce, Worcester sauce, lemon juice, cooked beans and courgettes with their buttery cooking liquid. Stir well. Season with salt and pepper to taste. Add the cubed fish and return to a very gentle heat for 10-15 minutes to cook the fish without breaking it up. Pipe creamed potato round the edge of a large ovenproof dish, or individual dishes, and fill with the fish mixture. Finish in the oven or under the grill until thoroughly heated. Serve with triangles of buttered toast.

BAKED PLAICE WITH SEAFOOD STUFFING

Jane Chapman, landlady of the Ship Inn at Axmouth, Devon, sent this fish and seafood recipe.

INGREDIENTS (PER PORTION)

1 fillet plaice

1 desertspoon crabmeat

8 peeled prawns

White sauce with added:

Fish stock

White wine

Fresh dill

Ground nutmeg

METHOD

Roll a fillet of plaice round a dessertspoon of crabmeat mixed with 8 peeled prawns. Cover with a white sauce made using milk and fish stock, flavoured with a little white wine and fresh dill. Either microwave for 2-3 minutes or bake in the centre of a hot oven (220°C, 425°F, gas mark 7) for 20 minutes. Grate a little nutmeg over the top and serve with croquette potatoes and a salad garnish.

QUICK FRIED SQUID WITH CHILLIES AND GARLIC

Gavin Crocker, landlord/chef at the Bull Inn, Cavendish in Suffolk, came up with this tongue-tingling recipe for squid.

INGREDIENTS (SERVES TWO)

750 g (1½ lb) fresh medium squid

2 green chillies, sliced

3 cloves garlic, minced or chopped

Flour

Salt

METHOD

Clean squid by removing beak from head reserving tentacles; open body tube by running knife down one side, remove backbone and rinse under cold water. Score flesh in a criss-cross pattern; cut into 3.5 cm x 3.5 cm (1½" x 1½") pieces. Coat in seasoned flour and deep fry at 190°C for 2 minutes. Heat wok until smoking, add 1 tablespoon oil, toss in garlic and chillies. Add squid and salt. Stir fry for 1 minute and serve with green salad and fresh lemon.

HERITAGE PUBS OF GREAT BRITAIN

It is still possible to enjoy real ale in sight of great craftsmanship and skill. What finer legacy for today's drinkers? Feast your eyes and toast the architects and builders from times past. This full colour collectible is a photographic record of some of the finest pub interiors in Britain. Many of the pubs included have been chosen from CAMRA's national inventory of pub interiors which should be saved at all costs. It is a collector's item. As such it is presented on heavy, gloss-art paper in a sleeved hard back format. The pub interiors have been photographed by architectural specialist Mark Bolton and described in words by pub expert James Belsey.

Heritage Pubs of Great Britain
by Mark Bolton and James Belsey
144 pages hard back   Price: £16.99
Available only from CAMRA – call 01727 867201 (overseas +44 1727 867201) to place credit card orders or send a cheque for £16.99 made out to 'CAMRA' and send it to:
CAMRA, 230 Hatfield Road, St Albans, Herts, AL1 4LW, UK

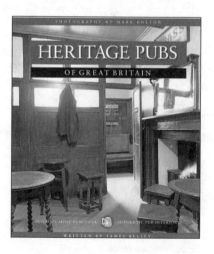

MEAT,
POULTRY
AND GAME

LAMB IN ORANGE AND ROSEMARY GRAVY

A simple but effective way of cooking lamb, from Julia Kingsford, landlady of the Fox & Hounds at Watlington in Oxfordshire.

INGREDIENTS (PER PORTION)

225 g (8 oz) boneless leg of lamb steak
1 cup fresh orange juice
Crushed garlic
½ tspn fresh rosemary leaves
Small amount of lamb stock
Freshly ground mixed peppercorns
1 tspn brown sugar

METHOD

Pan fry lamb steak in butter until rare/medium rare. Add fresh orange juice, crushed garlic, ½ tspn rosemary leaves, a small amount of lamb stock, freshly ground pepper and 1 tspn brown sugar. Braise the lamb in the gravy until just pink – the gravy will thicken with the pan juices. Serve with new potatoes or herby mash and fresh vegetables.

LAMB PIE

"This is not my original recipe. It was given to me by a local woman whose family recipe it was. I think we should save these recipes and use them before they disappear forever. Apparently it was popular in the 18th century." – Jan Turner, landlady of the Hare and Hound, Fosse Cross, Glos.

INGREDIENTS
(SERVES FOUR TO SIX)

750 g (1½ lbs) minced lamb

Rosemary

750 g (1½ lbs) minced ham

750 g (1½ lbs) shortcrust pastry

2 large onions, chopped

Beaten egg to glaze

750 g (1½ lbs) cooking apples

Sesame seeds

Butter

Oil

Seasoning

Cornflour

METHOD

Sweat the chopped onions in a little butter and oil. Remove half the onions and reserve. Add minced lamb to onions left in pan and fry gently until juices run out; add seasoning and half a pint of water and thicken with a little cornflour. Remove from pan and set aside. Return rest of onions to saucepan, add ham, and repeat process without salt. Meanwhile, peel, quarter and slice apples and blanche briefly in boiling water; drain. Line pie dish with pastry, spread lamb mixture over the bottom, put ham mixture on top, sprinkle generously with fresh or dried rosemary and finish by piling apples on top. Cover with pastry lid, brush with egg, sprinkle with sesame seeds and bake until golden brown in a medium oven (190°C, 375°F, gas mark 5).

LAVA LAMB (IN PASTRY CASE)

The Old Black Lion at Hay-on-Wye, Hereford, has a well-deserved reputation for fine food. Their chef, Miss W. Parton, sent her interpretation of a dish using local products.

INGREDIENTS
(SERVES 5+)

1 leg of lamb skinned and boned with gristle removed inside and out

Stuffing

2 medium onions, chopped

equal amount of chopped mushrooms

225 g (8 oz) fresh breadcrumbs

approx 100 g (4 oz) butter

225 g (8 oz) lavabread (seaweed, available from delicatessens)

Seasoning

Pastry

Just under 300 ml (½ pint) water

175 g (6 oz) lard

½ tspn salt

500 g (16 oz) plain flour

METHOD

Gently fry onions and mushrooms in butter until soft; stir in lavabread; using fork mix in breadcrumbs keeping the mixture as light as possible and using more butter if required. Stuff leg of lamb and tie securely with string; cover with 50 g (2 oz) butter and roast in prewarmed oven at 170°C, 325°F, gas mark 3 for 30 minutes. Pastry: Melt fat and water in pan, stir in flour and salt and knead thoroughly (adding another sprinkle of flour if necessary). Put in a warm, turned-off oven to rest for around 30 minutes. Remove string from meat, drain off juices and remove surplus stuffing. Put a little stuffing above and below the meat, cover the whole thing with pastry using hands to mould it, and glaze with beaten egg. Roast in slightly warmer oven (180°C, 350°F, gas mark 4) for a further 30 minutes or slightly longer until the meat is cooked through and the pastry golden brown.

HONEY AND MUSTARD GLAZED LAMB

At the Green Dragon in Cockleford, near Cheltenham, Glos, they create delicious meals from simple ingredients.

INGREDIENTS
("SERVES TWO HUNGRY, FOUR NOT HUNGRY")

500 g (1 lb) diced English leg of lamb

4 tblspns honey

1 large onion, chopped

Salt and pepper to taste

300 ml (½ pint) dry white wine

600 ml (1 pint) of stock made from the lamb bone

3 tblspns coarse grain mustard

Beurre manié (butter mixed with flour to form a roux)

Watercress to garnish

Broccoli

METHOD

Lightly fry the lamb with the onion to seal; add mustard, wine and honey; simmer, uncovered, to reduce liquid slightly. Add stock and simmer gently until lamb is tender (50-60 minutes). Thicken with beurre manié while stirring gently. Season to taste. At the pub they serve it with fluffy white rice, garnished with watercress, and crunchy broccoli.

LAMPLE PIE

Here's a regional recipe for a lamb and apple dish from the Harrow at Sevenoaks in Kent, which dates back at least 100 years.

INGREDIENTS

(A LARGE QUANTITY – ENOUGH TO FREEZE A COUPLE OF UNBAKED PIES. FOR ONE LARGE PIE USE HALF THE INGREDIENTS AND COOK FOR AROUND 30 MINUTES)

1 kg (2 lbs) puff pastry
100 g (4 oz) plain flour
600 ml (1 pint) milk
450g (1 lb) onions
Salt & pepper
2.25 kg (5 lbs) lean diced lamb
450g (1 lb) bramley apples
1.2 litres (2 pints) dry cider
75 g (3 oz) butter
Calvados
Egg wash

METHOD

Brown and seal the meat in the butter and then sprinkle on the flour to coat the meat. Add milk and stir until a light sauce is formed with the flour, then pour in the cider. Add the peeled, cored and coarsely chopped apples together with the chopped onion and seasoning. Stir, cover and simmer for 1½ hours. Allow this filling to cool and then divide between individual pie dishes, top each dish with apple slices and sprinkle with calvados. Roll out the pastry and top pie dishes. Brush with egg wash and bake in a hot oven (200°C, 400°F, gas mark 6) for approx 20 minutes.

DALESMAN'S PIE

Why do so many pubs put puff pastry topping on pies? We don't see enough shortcrust pastry – and even rarer is a suet crust pastry which is a delicious element of this thoroughly traditional Dalesman's Pie from Elizabeth Holt at the Moorcock Inn, Blacko in Lancs.

INGREDIENTS

450 g (1 lb) self-raising flour

450 g (1 lb) mixed root vegetables (carrots, swede,parsnips), cubed

225 g (8 oz) shredded suet

1 tspn salt

1 stick celery, sliced

Cold water to mix

Pinch of rosemary

1 kg (2 lbs) lamb shoulder, cubed

Seasoning

2 medium onions (sliced)

300 ml (½) pint red wine

METHOD

Mix flour, shredded suet and salt, then add enough cold water to form into suet crust pastry. Put all the other ingredients into a pan adding enough water to cover and simmer until tender then thicken with a little cornflour and water. Allow to cool, then pour into a pie dish with enough liquor to almost cover; top with rolled out suet crust pastry and bake in a hot oven (220°C, 425°F, gas mark 7) for around 30 minutes until the pastry is risen and golden brown (it soaks up the rich stock beautifully).

BAKED LAMB WITH ROSEMARY

It's not unusual to spike leg of lamb with rosemary but here is a fruity twist from the Red Lion at Raithby-by-Spilsby, Lincs. I particularly like the dog's involvement!

INGREDIENTS
(SERVES SIX-EIGHT)

1 leg of lamb

1 jar redcurrant jelly

1 pot sour cream (or yoghurt)

1 heaped dstspn chopped fresh rosemary

1 dstspn cornflour

METHOD

Cut lamb into thick slices, about 5 cm x 7.5 cm (2" x 3"). Throw bone to dog (who will disappear). Arrange lamb slices in baking tray. Beat together redcurrant jelly, sour cream or yoghurt, and rosemary into a thick, pink, prickly purée, and push between lamb slices. Bake in pre-heated moderate oven at 180°C, 350°F, gas mark 4 for 1 hour. Divide lamb slices on to serving plates; thicken pan juices with cornflour if wished and pour over lamb. Serve with buttered parsnips and peas.

BRAISED BEEF IN HONEY AND GINGER

The menu at the Sun Inn, a historic one-time mansion at Feering in Essex, is a romp through the traditional and the opulent with a Maltese flavour through landlord Charlie Scicluna, created by his wife, Kim.

INGREDIENTS
(SERVES FOUR)

1 tblspn oil

4 x 175 g (6 oz) beef braising steaks

1 tspn dried rosemary

2 cloves garlic, crushed

2½ cm (1") piece of fresh root ginger, peeled and chopped

100 g (4 oz) mushrooms, sliced

2 tblspns soy sauce

1 tblspn clear honey

150 ml (half pint) beef stock

Black pepper to taste

Half to 1 tblspn cornflour mixed with water

METHOD

Heat oil, and brown steaks on both sides. Lay steaks in ovenproof dish large enough to take them in a single layer. Mix remaining ingredients together except for the cornflour. Bring to the boil, then add cornflour until sauce has thickened. Pour over beef, cover and cook in the oven for up to 2 hours at 170°C, 325°F, gas mark 3.

STEAK CAMERON

A pithy recipe with a Scottish flavour from Alistair Veitch at the Castlecary House Hotel, Castlecary in Strathclyde.

INGREDIENTS
(PER PORTION)

225 g (8 oz) fillet steak

Double cream

Oatmeal for coating

1 slice of bread, crust removed

Butter for frying

1 slice of mature Cheddar (Alistair uses Crowdie) to cover bread

½ a small onion, sliced

1 double Scotch whisky

METHOD

Coat steak in oatmeal and fry in butter to taste; remove and keep warm. Fry onion in pan until soft then add whisky and bring to bubbling point, then stir in enough double cream to make a coating sauce; season to taste. In a separate pan fry the bread on one side in butter until golden brown. Place cheese on unfried side and place under a hot grill until bubbling. Place the steak on top and cover with the whisky sauce.

EVESHAM PIE

Known for their well-executed English dishes using superb ingredients, the Crown and Trumpet at Broadway in Worcestershire has sent this old-fashioned local dish.

INGREDIENTS
(SERVES FOUR)

600 ml (1 pint) beef stock

450 g (1 lb) plums

750 g (1½ lb) stewing steak, cubed

25 g (1 oz) seasoned flour

50 ml (2 fl oz) oil

300 ml (½ pint) plum wine

2 tspns sugar

450g (1 lb) flaky pastry

METHOD

Bring the stock and wine to the boil, pour over the stoned plums and leave to soak for 1 hour. Coat the beef cubes with flour. Heat the oil in a saucepan, add the beef and fry for 5 minutes or until brown all over. Strain the stock from the plums and add to the meat, bring to the boil and simmer until the liquid thickens, add sugar and plums and cook for 1 ¾ hours or until the meat is tender. Pour into a pie dish, cover with flaky pastry and cook in the oven at 220°C, 425°F, gas mark 7, for a further 25 minutes.

THE BUTTERLEIGH INN BURGER

There's a world of difference between home-made and shop-bought burgers. Here is an example of the former, made at Butterleigh Inn, Cullompton, Devon.

INGREDIENTS
(FOR AROUND EIGHT BURGERS)

1 kg (2 lbs) minced beef

2 medium-sized onions, finely chopped

125 g (4 oz) fresh breadcrumbs

1 dstspn made English mustard

1 dstspn Worcester sauce

1 dstspn salt

2 tspns ground pepper

150 ml (5 fl oz) milk

1 dstspn fresh chopped parsley

METHOD

Mix all ingredients thoroughly and press into a burger mould or shape by hand. Chill thoroughly before frying or grilling.

SUCKLING PIG ROASTED WITH HONEY AND GINGER

Here is a really impressive centrepiece, with a hint of the Orient, from The Drovers Inn at East Linton, Lothian in Scotland.

INGREDIENTS

Suckling pig prepared by your butcher

Fresh ginger, small root

¼ jar Scottish honey

Seasoning

Mixed fresh herbs

4 tblspns oil

For honey and ginger jus

½ bottle red wine

Fresh ginger, small root

¼ jar Scottish honey

Small jar redcurrant jelly

Seasoning

15 g (½ oz) ham bouillon dissolved in 600 ml (1 pint) boiling water

Cornflour for thickening

METHOD

Mix ginger, honey, seasoning, herbs and oil and spread over suckling pig in a roasting tray then roast on a slow heat, 160°C, 325°F, gas mark 3, for 2½ hours or until tender, basting the pig until the skin is crisp. Make the jus by reducing the red wine, then add the rest of the ingredients, bring to the boil and thicken with cornflour. Serve pig on a hot platter with the fresh ginger and honey sauce.

SOMERSET PORK, HONEY AND WHOLEGRAIN MUSTARD HOT POT

Here is a local dish combining pork with cider, mustard and honey from Wayne Dowding of the Bird in Hand at Saltford near Bristol.

INGREDIENTS
(SERVES FOUR)

1.5 kg (3 lbs) pork
1 medium onion, chopped
75 g (3 oz) carrot, diced
50 g (2 oz) celery, chopped
3 tblspns honey
2 tblspns wholegrain mustard
50 g (2 oz) mushrooms
1-2 tblspns plain four
1 dstspn paprika
600 ml (1 pint) light meat or vegetable stock
Salt
Cracked black pepper
1 bay leaf
Red wine to taste
150 ml (¼ pint) traditional cider (Thatchers!)

METHOD

Place diced pork in 1 tblspn of hot oil; seal and brown. Add chopped carrots, onion, bay leaf, celery and mushrooms and sweat for 2-3 minutes. Add flour to make a roux, then stir in paprika. Add stock slowly, then stir in the honey, wholegrain mustard, red wine and traditional cider. Season to taste and serve in small pots with fresh garden vegetables and minted new potatoes.

WHITE HORSE SOMERSET PORK

Here is a rich, Somerset dish using cider, from Anne Williamson at the White Horse Inn at Stogumber in Somerset.

INGREDIENTS
(SERVES FIVE-SIX)

1.5 kg (2½ lbs) diced pork
225 g (½ lb) button mushrooms
350 g (12 oz) onions
300 ml (½ pint) dry cider
300 ml (½ pint) milk
100 g (4 oz) clotted cream (double cream will do)
300 ml (½ pint) water.
1 tblspn cornflour

METHOD

Trim surplus fat from the pork, finely dice onions and marinade with the pork in cider and water for 1 hour, then simmer for 30 minutes. Slice the mushrooms, mix a level tblspn of cornflour with milk and add to the pork mix; simmer for a further 45 minutes stirring occasionally. When pork is tender remove from heat and slowly stir in the cream. Serve with potatoes and vegetables.

PORK ESCALOPE IN PERNOD

You'll always find something that bit different on the menu of the Maypole Inn at Long Preston, North Yorkshire, such as this recipe for pork with Pernod.

INGREDIENTS
(SERVES FOUR)

4 pork escalopes
1 small carton double cream
100 g (4 oz) sliced button mushrooms
3 tblspns Pernod
1 heaped tblspn fresh chopped basil (approx)
Seasoning
25 g (1 oz) butter
To serve:
Green noodles
Green salad

METHOD

Flatten pork escalopes and fry gently in butter until just cooked, turning frequently; remove and set aside. Add thinly sliced mushrooms and fresh chopped basil to taste to the pan and fry for a couple of minutes to blend the flavours. Remove from heat and stir in the Pernod and cream, then return pork to the pan and allow to bubble gently until the sauce thickens, seasoning with salt and pepper. Serve with noodles and green salad.

PORK ESCALOPE IN A CARAMELISED APPLE SAUCE

Here's a savoury application of the toffee apple principle from Halzephron Inn at Gunwalloe in Cornwall.

INGREDIENTS
(SERVES TWO)

1 large pork fillet

50 g (2 oz) butter

2 English eating apples

300 ml (½ pint) double cream

75 g (3 oz) demerara sugar

Flour, egg and breadcrumbs for coating

METHOD

Cut pork fillet into eight equal pieces; flatten into thin escalopes and dip in the flour, beaten egg and fresh breadcrumbs before frying in a small amount of butter for 4 minutes on each side. Keep warm.

To make the sauce: put the rest of the butter and demerara sugar in a saucepan and cook slowly until the sugar begins to caramelise. Add chopped slices of apple to the caramel and toss. Pour in double cream and bring to the boil then reduce for about 1 minute. The sauce should be of a coating consistency. Serve escalopes with sauce, new potatoes and mixed green salad.

HUMBLE PIE

Humble without being obsequious, this dish was sent by award-winners Edwin and Trudy Cheeseman from the Black Horse, Woburn.

INGREDIENTS

Diced vegetables

Cooking apples, thinly sliced

Diced pork

Home-made stuffing

Sausages cut in chunks (or small bangers)

Shortcrust pastry

METHOD

Form 1 cm (½") thick layers of each ingredient in an ovenproof dish: first vegetables, then pork and sausages, then cooking apples; then a layer of stuffing and finish with a layer of vegetables. Finally cover with pastry and bake for at least an hour at 190°C, 375°F, gas mark 5, covering pastry with foil if it starts to get too brown.

PORK CONOR

Here is another recipe from the picturesque Hillside Bar, Hillsborough.

INGREDIENTS
(SERVES SIX)

1 kg (2 lbs) pork steaks, cubed

1 small red pepper, diced

1 small green pepper, diced

50 g (2 oz) button mushrooms

½ onion, finely chopped

50 g (2 oz) butter

50 g (2 oz) flour

300 ml (½ pint) water

½ glass dry white wine

1 tspn mixed herbs

(200 ml) 7 fl oz cider

(200 ml) 7 fl oz cream

METHOD

Fry pork and onion in butter. Add flour and cook to light brown. Add water, wine and cider; stir in mushrooms, peppers and herbs. Transfer to casserole dish and cook in moderate oven for 45 minutes until pork is tender. Remove from oven, stir in cream and serve with a crisp green side salad.

BURTON HOUSE PIG'S FRY

I am grateful to the landlord at the Burton House Hotel in Boston for sending me the recipe for this Lincolnshire dish, because it embroiled him in a lively bar-room discussion on the many local variations. "I suppose Mrs Beeton would say, "Take one medium size pig and sauté gently!" he says.

INGREDIENTS
(FOR SIX PEOPLE)

| 450 g (1 lb) belly pork, sliced |
| 175 g (6 oz) pig's liver sliced |
| 100 g (4 oz) pig's kidney, chopped |
| 1 Lincolnshire sausage per person |
| 1 sliced heart (optional) |
| 2 medium onions, sliced. |
| Real ale |
| 25 g (1 oz) dripping |
| Seasoned flour |

METHOD

Sauté onions in dripping until brown; coat meats in seasoned flour, then fry to seal and brown; place with onions in casserole dish and add a small amount of liquid (they use Bateman's bitter). Simmer in centre of medium oven until tender. Grill sausages and add to the dish for the last 20 minutes.

BACON PUDDING

A dish to revive weary travellers is Linda Redman's Bacon Pudding which she serves at the Travellers Rest at Newton near Fareham in Hants. She believes it originates from Kent.

INGREDIENTS
(SERVES SIX-EIGHT)

275 g (10 oz) flour
150 g (5 oz) shredded suet
750 g (1½ lbs) streaky bacon
1 large onion
Large pinch of sage (dried or fresh)
Salt

METHOD

Pastry
Sift flour and salt into a bowl; add suet and enough water to make a soft rolling dough; roll out dough.

Filling
Cut bacon into 2.5 cm (1") pieces, sprinkle onto dough; add finely chopped onion and sprinkle sage; roll up dough (as for roly-poly pudding). Wrap in a cloth lined with lining paper to prevent sticking. Put directly into boiling water, and cook for 1½-2 hours, turning the water down but keeping it on the brisk simmer and adding more hot water if necessary. Serve with boiled potatoes and vegetables. This dish can be cooked as a pudding in a basin if preferred.

RHINELAND PIE

Chef Rotraud Palmer at the Old Tom in St. Aldates, Oxford, hails from Germany and has sent me this cheap and delicious dish from her homeland. She keeps threatening to leave, so I'm glad to have the recipe.

INGREDIENTS

250 g (8 oz) smoked bacon, chopped
500 g (1 lb) onions, chopped and fried in butter
Pinch of mixed herbs
Small pot sour cream
3 eggs
2 tblspns single cream
300 ml (½ pint) milk
Shortcrust pastry to line quiche dish

METHOD

Line quiche dish with pastry. Mix the bacon, fried onions, herbs and sour cream together and spread over pastry. Then mix eggs, single cream and milk and pour over. Bake in pre-heated oven at 190°C, 375°F, gas mark 5 for approx 45 minutes, until cooked through and golden brown.

ALISON'S ALSTON PIE

Here is a splendid recipe devised by Alison Clark at the Miners Arms, Nenthead, near Alston in Cumbria, using her local produce and appearing in her own recipe book.

INGREDIENTS (SERVES SIX)

250 g (8 oz) Cumberland sausage

175 g (6 oz) Alston cheese (or mature Cheddar)

1 large onion, peeled and quartered

1 tspn Cumberland wholegrain mustard

300 ml (½ pint) milk

Salt and pepper

6 eggs

450 g (1 lb) shortcrust pastry

4 tblspns fromage frais

Beaten egg to glaze

METHOD

Grill sausage; cool and slice. Put onion, milk, eggs, fromage frais and mustard, and dash of salt and pepper, in a food processor and mix for a couple of minutes (or finely chop onion and whisk with the other ingredients). Line a flan dish with half the pastry, covering this with the sliced sausage. Pour on the processed mixture, then sprinkle grated cheese over the top. Roll out the remaining pastry and cover the pie; glaze with egg wash and cook in a moderate oven (200°C, 400°F, gas mark 6).

SAUSAGE PIE AND PICKLES

Here is a "quickie" sausage pie from the Victoria in Lincoln, former East Midlands CAMRA Pub of the Year.

INGREDIENTS
(SERVES FOUR)

450 g (11b) shortcrust pastry
225 g (8 oz) Lincolnshire sausagemeat
2 large onions, sliced and boiled
Fresh sage & parsley
Egg wash
Pickle:
1 large onion,, finely sliced
1/2 cucumber, peeled and finely sliced
Malt vinegar

METHOD

Roll out half the pastry and line a quiche dish. Fill with sausagemeat, cover with boiled onions, sprinkle with fresh sage and parsley, top with the rest of the pastry, brush with beaten egg and bake slowly for an hour in a moderate oven. Serve warm with the onions and cucumber, which have been soaked overnight in the malt vinegar.

FARMBRIDGE PIE

Cook Ros Gibson got used to cooking her local dish Fambridge Pie in larger quantities at the Anchor in Fambridge, Essex but says these are approx quantities for a family-size meal.

INGREDIENTS

450 g (1 lb)shortcrust pastry

300 ml (½ pint) fairly thick white sauce

225 g (8 oz) cooked, diced chicken

1 large, diced gammon steak

1 beaten egg

175 g (6 oz) sausagemeat

50 g (2 oz) stuffing or 1 tblspn fresh chopped herbs and 4 tblspns fresh breadcrumbs bound with egg into a fairly stiff mix.

100 g (4 oz) mushrooms

METHOD

Add chicken, gammon and mushrooms to white sauce; combine stuffing or herb/crumb mix with sausagemeat. Line a 23 cm (9") pie plate with rolled out pastry. Spread enough chicken mix to cover pastry; spread sausage mix on top and cover with remaining chicken mix. Top with pastry, glaze with egg and bake in pre-heated oven (200°C, 400°F, gas mark 6) for approx 25 minutes until golden brown. Serve hot or cold.

HUNTINGDON FIDGET PIE

Karen Billows of the Free Press in Cambridge shared her recipe for a local pie from the past, which always went down well in the pub.

INGREDIENTS
(SERVES FOUR)

225 g (8 oz) plain flour

100 g (4 oz) butter – diced

Salt and pepper

225 g (8 oz) back bacon – roughly chopped

1 medium onion – roughly chopped

225 g (8 oz) cooking apples - peeled, cored and roughly chopped

1 tblspn chopped parsley

150 ml (¼ pint) medium-dry cider

1 egg – beaten, for the glaze

25 g (1 oz) flour

METHOD

For the pastry, sift 225 g (8 oz) flour and a pinch of salt into a bowl. Rub in the butter until the mixture resembles breadcrumbs. Add enough cold water to mix to a firm dough. Gather the dough into a ball and knead lightly. Wrap it in foil and chill in the refrigerator for 30 minutes. Meanwhile, combine the bacon, onion and apples. Add the parsley and season to taste. Roll out the pastry to provide a lid and to line a 600 ml (1 pint) pie dish, put in the bacon mixture. Blend 25 g (1 oz) flour with the cider, a little at a time, then pour into the pie dish. Place the lid on top and press to seal. Knock up and flute the edge. Make a diagonal cross in the centre almost to the edges of the dish, then fold the pastry back to reveal the filling. Brush the pastry with the egg. Bake at 190°C, 375°F, gas mark 5, for about 45 minutes or until cooked.

SUPREME OF CHICKEN WITH A SALAD OF MARINATED PEPPERS

This is an excellent and colourful Mediterranean-style hot salad from the deliciously varied menu of the Silver Plough at Pitton, Wiltshire.

INGREDIENTS
(SERVES FOUR)

4 small assorted peppers (ie green, yellow, red and orange)

2 large free-range chicken breasts

Olive oil

Basalmic vinegar

Fresh tarragon

Salt and pepper

METHOD

To make the salad

Halve and de-seed peppers and place skin-side down on a baking tray; sprinkle with olive oil and balsamic vinegar and season well. Roast in a hot oven at 230°C, 450°F, gas mark 8 for around 10 minutes until the skin blisters and the peppers soften. Cool and rub with a damp teatowel to remove the skin, and cover with a vinaigrette made of three parts olive oil to one part balsamic vinegar. (Can be made a few days in advance).

To cook chicken

Remove skin from the breasts and poach in a little water or stock for 7-10 minutes until thoroughly cooked. In a shallow sauté pan, reheat the pepper salad. Arrange peppers on plates topped with chicken breast cut into strips, pour vinaigrette over and garnish with the chopped tarragon.

OLDBURY CHICKEN

From Alex de la Torre at the Anchor Inn, Oldbury-on-Severn, near Bristol, comes a dish in which chicken instead of pork is flavoured with apple and calvados.

INGREDIENTS
(SERVES SIX)

6 chicken breasts

250 g (8 oz) button mushrooms, wiped

175 g (6 oz) double cream

½ litre (16 fl oz) still, unsweetened apple juice

3 measures calvados

1 dstspn brown sugar

Salt and pepper

Oil (for frying)

Flour (approx 4 tblspns)

METHOD

Wipe chicken breasts and coat in seasoned flour. Heat oil in a large frying pan, add chicken and fry on both sides until golden brown (5-10 minutes). Transfer chicken to a casserole dish; add apple juice and whole mushrooms, cover and cook in pre-heated oven at 180°C, 350°F, gas mark 4 for around 20 minutes. Add calvados and sugar, stir in and taste, adjusting seasoning as required; return to oven until cooked (approx 15 minutes). Remove chicken and keep warm. Reduce sauce by simmering for 10 minutes, add cream and continue simmering for 5 minutes. Pour over chicken breasts and serve with fresh green vegetables and new potatoes.

CHICKEN SUPREME IN SHERRY

Steve Thomas, the chef at Oaklands pub/hotel in Gorstage near Weaverham, Cheshire, says: "This is very simple, anyone can do it."

INGREDIENTS (PER PORTION)

1 boneless breast of chicken, cut into long, thin strips and marinated in a tblspn of sherry for at least an hour
25 g (1 oz) butter
1 heaped tblspn chopped parsley
1 small onion, finely sliced
50 g (2 oz) mushrooms, finely sliced
1 small carrot cut into julienne strips
Garlic salt
1 tblspn sherry

METHOD

Drain excess marinade from chicken, season strips with a little garlic salt and gently fry with sliced onion in butter until sealed on all sides. Add marinade drained from chicken plus another tablespoon of sherry; lower heat and cover; cook gently for around 5 minutes. Add mushrooms and carrots, replace lid and continue simmering gently for a further 5 minutes. Spoon onto boiled rice and garnish with chopped parsley.

ROMAN HAZELNUT CHICKEN

The Hare and Hounds at Foss Cross, Glos, combines the old and the new on its menu. Here is landlady Jan Turner's recipe for Roman Hazelnut Chicken.

INGREDIENTS (SERVES SIX)

6 chicken portions
½ bottle of medium white wine
Dried chives
Cornflour
300 ml (½ pint) chicken stock
125 ml (4 fl oz) cream
1 handful chopped hazelnuts

METHOD

Place chicken portions in a large, shallow baking dish; pour wine over and sprinkle generously with dried chives. Bake in a medium oven until chicken is just cooked, then drain juices into a saucepan. Add chicken stock, cream and salt and pepper to taste. Heat to simmering point and allow it to cook down a little, then thicken with cornflour if liked. Toss in a handful of chopped hazelnuts, pour over chicken, and return to oven until browned.

CHICKEN APRICOT

From the Butchers Arms at Alltwen, Glamorgan, comes Chicken Apricot with garlic potatoes to accompany.

INGREDIENTS (PER PORTION)

1 chicken breast, diced

50 g (2 oz) each of red pepper, green pepper and mushrooms, diced

Half a small onion, chopped

1-2 apricots

1 measure apricot brandy

A little single cream

METHOD

Sauté vegetables in butter and add diced chicken; sauté for a few minutes until chicken is cooked. Add 1-2 chopped apricots, depending on size, and flame with apricot brandy; add cream and cook gently until sauce thickens.

BARBARY DUCK OAK STYLE

Award-winning landlady, Eileen Hines of the Royal Oak, Lostwithiel, in Cornwall, has had dishes named after her, but this tasty duck meal is named for the pub on an old smuggling route.

INGREDIENTS (SERVES TWO)

One 1¾ kg (3½ lbs) Barbary duck

2 tblspns honey

½ tspn garlic paste

Pinch of five-spice powder

½ an orange

2 tblspns soy sauce

½ tspn ground ginger

Salt

300 ml (½ pint) water

Sauce

1 orange

300 ml (½ pint) water

½ tspn ground ginger

Stock (from duck giblets)

METHOD

Preheat oven to 180°C, 350°F, gas mark 4. Scald skin of duck with boiling water and leave to dry. Mix honey, soy sauce, garlic paste, ginger and five-spice powder to make a paste. Prick skin of duck all over and rub with salt. Squeeze orange over duck then brush the paste well into the skin. Leave to stand for 1 hour. Place duck on a wire rack in a meat tray with the water and roast for 2 hours, turning frequently. To make the sauce, grate rind of orange, reserving the juice. Simmer the rind in the water until tender, add the juice, ginger and 4 tblspns stock; simmer briskly uncovered until thickened.

Eileen serves it as half a duck per portion, the breast and rib bones removed, or you can carve slices from the joint. Decorate with slices of orange, serve with the sauce and fresh vegetables.

ROQUEFORT AND VENISON CRUMBLE

Christine and Martin Baucutt of the Shepherds Inn at Melmerby, Cumbria, share the cooking, and have won food awards. Here is their recipe for teaming English game with two continental cheeses.

INGREDIENTS (SERVES 10)

2 shoulders venison (preferably roe deer)

6 juniper berries, crushed

1 bottle red wine

2 cloves garlic, crushed

3 sticks celery, chopped

3 bouquet garni

1 kg (2 lbs) belly pork cut into small chunks

2-3 bay leaves

Salt and black pepper

4 medium onions cut into rings

1 kg (2 lbs) sliced carrots

Cornflour to thicken

300 g (12 oz) plain flour

300 g (12 oz) wholewheat flour

225 g (8 oz) butter

Pinch of salt and black pepper

150 g (6 oz) Mozzarella, grated

75 g (3 oz) whole hazelnuts

75 g (3 oz) cashew nuts

10 thin slices Roquefort

METHOD

Remove venison from bones in ½" chunks. Marinade in wine with berries, onions, celery and garlic for 24 hours. Cook bones in water to produce a rich stock; allow to cool, and strain. Place venison and marinade in saucepan with bouquet garni, bay leaves and pepper, cover and simmer slowly. After 1 hour add pork and carrots. Simmer until venison and pork are tender. Top up the reducing liquor with venison stock. Remove berries and bouquet garni and thicken with cornflour. Season to taste. Put into a large wide casserole or pie dish and allow to cool. Make crumble by mixing flours with salt and pepper. Add butter and rub to fine crumbs. Stir in Mozzarella and nuts, and spread over the top of the meat. Top with Roquefort slices and bake in a hot oven (220°C, 425°F, gas mark 7) for up to 30 minutes, until the meat mixture has reheated and the crumble/Roquefort is brown and bubbling.

JUGGED YORKSHIRE HARE

The enthusiasm of Susan Richardson, licensee and cook at the Star Inn in Weaverthorpe, North Yorks, is always catching. Here is her recipe for hare - farmers bring them to the door.

INGREDIENTS
(SERVES FOUR)

1 large hare (jointed)
2 onions, finely sliced
2 carrots, chopped
2 sticks celery, chopped
1 tblspn tomato purée
2 cloves garlic, crushed
Grated rind of 1 lemon
300 ml (½ pint) red wine
2 tblspns port
50 g (2 oz) bacon, chopped
50 g (2 oz) seasoned flour
Bay leaf or bouquet garni
Beef stock or water

METHOD

Wipe the hare joints and coat in seasoned flour; seal quickly in oil and butter in a heavy pan, then set aside. In same pan sauté onions until transparent, then add garlic, carrots, celery and bacon. Return hare to pan. Mix red wine, tomato purée and lemon rind then pour over meat, adding enough beef stock or water to just cover. Add bay leaf or bouquet garni. Cover and cook slowly, either on top of the stove or in the oven, for approx 2 hours, until the hare is tender. Adjust seasoning, add port wine and serve with creamed potatoes, root vegetables "and a healthy appetite", adds Susan.

CASSEROLE OF LOCAL GAME
(BEWARE OF SHOT!)

A rural game casserole from the Running Horses, Mickleham, Surrey, where they are kept supplied by keen local sportsmen and do all the preparation themselves. You can get your butcher to do it for you, or get most of the ingredients ready-prepared in the supermarket, though you may have to substitute rabbit for hare, and the flavour won't be so robust.

INGREDIENTS

Selection of pheasant, hare, venison, partridge, grouse etc. usually supplied by local sportsmen (except the venison, of course)

For each 500 g (1 lb) meat:

100 g (4 oz) mushrooms, diced

100 g (4 oz) onions, diced

50 g (2 oz) tomato purée

50 g (2 oz) flour

600 ml (1 pint) beef stock

1 tspn redcurrant jelly

50 g (2 oz) beef dripping

METHOD

Skin, pluck, and gut all the game after hanging for one week. Remove all meat from the bones and cut into 1" cubes. Put in container with bay leaves, peppercorns and just cover with red wine. Refrigerate for two days. On the third day drain wine from meat and retain. Fry meat in dripping in hot skillet until golden brown, then transfer to casserole. Fry onions and mushrooms in the same skillet and add to casserole. Stir flour into remaining fat and cook slowly, stirring, for 5 minutes; add stock and wine from marinade slowly, then stir in tomato purée with redcurrant jelly, bring to the boil, pour over meat and cook in a moderate oven 190°C, 375°F, gas mark 5 for 1½ hours until tender. Remove grease from top and serve with fresh vegetables and a heart-shaped crouton.

RABBIT PIE WITH LEMON AND HERBS

Heather Humphreys, now at the Rising Sun at Woodland in Devon, is an extremely accomplished cook, her menu biased towards traditional English cuisine. Here is her recipe for one of her most popular traditional dishes.

INGREDIENTS

2 wild rabbits (or equivalent rabbit portions)
2 rashers streaky bacon, de-rinded and chopped
1 medium onion, finely chopped
1 tblspn finely chopped fresh herbs
Grated rind of half a lemon
Salt and freshly ground black pepper to taste
A good pinch of ground mace
1 dstspn plain flour
450 g (1 lb) flaky pastry

METHOD

Cover rabbits with water, simmer for 1-1½ hours until tender, drain, reserving stock. Remove meat from bones and cut into small pieces. Mix with remaining ingredients and moisten well with stock. Roll out half the pastry and line a pie dish. Fill with the rabbit mixture. Top with the remaining pastry and brush with egg and milk. Bake in a pre-heated hot oven (220°C, 425°F, gas mark 7) for 25-30 minutes until the pastry is risen and golden brown.

NORTHUMBRIA RABBIT CASSEROLE

Ray Johnson, former teacher turned publican, sent this recipe from the Fox and Hounds at Wylam near Newcastle - note the local black pudding and mead from Lindisfarne.

INGREDIENTS

1 fresh skinned rabbit

225 g (8 oz) button onions

175 g (6 oz) button mushrooms

100 g (4 oz) strips of bacon

100 g (4 oz) black pudding

50 g (2 oz) flour

just over 50 g (2 oz) fat

Pinch of fresh herbs

1½ oz tomato purée

Stock

Marinade:

300 ml (½ pint) mead

4 tblspns oil

Sprig each of thyme and parsley

100 g (4 oz) chopped carrots, onion and celery

Chopped clove of garlic

12 peppercorns

Pinch of salt.

METHOD

Mix marinade ingredients together. Joint rabbit and place in marinade for a few hours or overnight. Remove rabbit and chopped vegetables and fry in hot fat; add the flour and brown gently. Add tomato purée, marinade liquor and around 150 ml (¼ pint) of stock; bring to boil; add herbs. Place in a covered casserole and cook in a moderate oven (180°C, 350°F, gas mark 4) for approx 1 hour until tender. Meanwhile cook button onions in salted water. Place rabbit on serving dish and keep warm. Fry strips of bacon, cubed black pudding and button mushrooms. Strain cooking sauce over rabbit, garnish with bacon, black pudding, mushrooms and button onions; sprinkle with chopped parsley and serve redcurrant jelly separately.

HAYTOR RABBIT CASSEROLE

Just to show how different a rabbit casserole can be depending on where you eat it, here is one version as served at the Rock Inn on Dartmoor using cider and cream.

INGREDIENTS
(FOR FOUR)

Olive oil

1 onion (peeled and finely chopped)

175 g (6 oz) smoked bacon (rinds removed and diced)

1 kg (2 lbs) jointed rabbit

Flour for coating

Salt and black pepper

2 tblspns tomato purée

100 g (4 oz) tomato concassé

450 ml (¼ pint) dry cider

Bouquet garni

3 carrots (thinly sliced)

3 sticks celery (finely chopped)

225 g (8 oz) whole button mushrooms

Double cream for finishing

Chopped parsley

METHOD

Heat 2-3 tblspns of olive oil, add onion, celery, carrot and bacon. Cook until golden brown, coat rabbit in seasoned flour, add to casserole and colour well on all sides. Stir in tomato purée and concassé and cider, bring slowly to the boil, stirring constantly. Add the bouquet garni, cover casserole and cook in moderate oven (180°C, 350°F, gas mark 4) for 1-1½ hrs until rabbit is tender. Add whole mushrooms, cook for a further 5-10 minutes then remove from oven. Finish with cream, garnish with freshly chopped parsley. Serve with fresh seasoned vegetables.

PIGEON AND BLACK CHERRY CASSEROLE

Trudey Duke, the landlord's mum, cooks the dinners at the Plough Inn, East Stratton, Hants. Here is an inexpensive but rather sophisticated supper dish.

INGREDIENTS (SERVES EIGHT)

4 plump pigeons

3 tblspns mixed herbs (sage, thyme, lemon balm, bay leaf and rosemary)

10 juniper berries

300 ml (½ pint) red wine

4 rashers streaky bacon

2 medium oranges

225 g (8 oz) fresh or tinned black cherries

2 medium red onions, sliced

METHOD

Marinate the pigeons overnight in red wine, juniper berries, juice from both oranges and zest from one. Next day, put sliced onions in the bottom of a casserole, add pigeons breast down, and put a bacon rasher over each. Sprinkle over herbs and add wine marinade. Cook in a slow oven (140°C, 300°F, gas mark 2) for at least 3 hours until tender. Remove pigeons from casserole and thicken stock slightly if necessary with cornflour. Carefully cut breasts from pigeons and place in stock along with fresh or tinned cherries, return to the oven and cook for a further 30 minutes.

WOOD PIGEON GATEAUX WITH PRUNE MAYONNAISE

Champion cook Martin Mitchell has won several awards at the Johnsburn House, Balerno, near Edinburgh, by bringing a new twist to traditional Scottish tastes. Here is his version of pigeon pie.

INGREDIENTS
(SERVES FOUR)

4 sheets filo pastry
8 large firm tomatoes
4 small pigeons
A sprinkling of pine kernels
1 small tin prunes (stoned)
4 leaves fresh basil
100 g (4 oz) thick mayonnaise
1 tblspn hazelnut oil
2 large washed potatoes

METHOD

Stamp four rounds from each sheet of filo and fry in butter until crisp. Remove breasts from pigeons with a sharp knife, then sauté until still slightly pink in the centre. Remove flesh from the tomatoes and bind with basil and hazelnut oil. Puree the prunes with mayonnaise. Slice the potatoes into fine matchsticks and deep fry. Spread the filo rounds with prune mayonnaise and add two fine slices of pigeon. Continue to build the gateaux, ending with a plain round of filo garnished with pine kernels. Surround the gateaux with mounds of matchstick potatoes and tomatoes and serve with a sauce made from pigeon leftovers.

VEGETARIAN

YVONNE'S BREAD PUDDING

Yvonne MacFarlane reached the national finals of a pub food competition while landlady at the Somerset Inn, Paulton in Somerset. Here is her recipe for a most unusual savoury bread pudding.

INGREDIENTS
(SERVES EIGHT)

A large crusty loaf (sliced, cut into triangles, crusts removed and reserved for breadcrumbs)

Garlic butter

Sauce

1 kg (2 lbs) tomatoes, skinned and chopped

4 medium onions, sliced

4-5 cloves garlic, crushed

3-4 tblspns fresh chopped basil

1 wineglass red wine

Cheddar cheese

6 egg yolks

900 ml (1½ pints) milk

5 tblspns stuffed olives, sliced

Olive oil for frying

METHOD

Spread bread triangles with garlic butter. Put a layer in the bottom of a 26 cm (10") baking tin, with sides at least 5 cm (2") deep. To make the sauce, sauté onions and garlic in a little olive oil, add tomatoes, red wine and basil, and simmer gently until the onions are soft; stir in sliced olives. Cover the first layer of bread with half the sauce; cover with thinly sliced Cheddar; spread a second layer of garlic bread, then the rest of the sauce and final layer of cheese. Whisk together eggs and milk and pour over. Cover with a generous layer of crumbs made from the bread crusts and grated cheese. Bake on the middle shelf of a moderate oven at 180°C, 350°F, gas mark 4 for 30-40 minutes, until egg custard is set. The pudding should be light and fluffy with a golden, crunchy top.

CRISPY FILO PARCEL OF WILD RICE AND LEEKS WITH A CHERRY TOMATO AND WINE SAUCE

Roger Payne, chef at the Rattlebone Inn, Sherston in Wilts, is always generous in sharing his gorgeous recipes. This is a deliciously tempting dish

INGREDIENTS
(SERVES SIX)

12 sheets filo pastry

225 g (8 oz) Canadian wild rice (cooked in vegetable stock for about 1 hour)

2 chopped onions

4 leeks (washed and chopped)

2 eggs

100 g (4 oz) butter

2 cloves garlic

450 g (1 lb) cherry tomatoes

300 ml (½ pint) good white wine (Chardonnay)

METHOD

Cook rice until soft, then drain. Fry rice and 1 chopped onion in oil and garlic, then add leeks and continue cooking until soft. Season with salt and black pepper, then bind with 2 eggs. When cool, roll into filo parcels, 2 sheets per portion, brushing melted butter between sheets. Bake in pre-heated oven at 220°C, 425°F, gas mark 7 for 20 minutes. For the sauce, fry remaining onion in a little butter with salt, pepper and pinch of sugar. Add wine and reduce, then add cherry tomatoes and simmer until soft; serve under the parcel.

LAVABREAD, LEEK AND CAERPHILLY CHEESE RISSOLES

Andrew Canning of the Clytha Arms near Abergavenny used traditional Welsh ingredients to create a thoroughly modern vegetarian dish.

INGREDIENTS (SERVES FOUR)

25 g (1 oz) grated Parmesan
½ tspn thyme
275 g (10 oz) farmhouse Caerphilly (grated)
2 tspns mustard powder
250 g (9 oz) fresh breadcrumbs
Generous pinch of salt
4 tblspns chopped leeks
Freshly ground black pepper
1 tblspn chopped spring onion
6 egg yolks (keep whites)
175 g (6 oz) lavabread (available tinned)
Oatmeal and extra breadcrumbs for coating
3 tblspns chopped parsley

METHOD

Mix together all ingredients apart from the oatmeal and extra breadcrumbs. Form into fishcake shapes, dip in oatmeal, then in the spare egg whites, then in fresh breadcrumbs and deep fry in medium hot fat until golden brown. Drain on kitchen paper and serve with home-made relish.

RICOTTA AND PEA PIE

The Sun Inn, a quite extraordinary historic pub at Feering in Essex has contributed several recipes, and here is one that vegetarians will love.

INGREDIENTS
(SERVES FOUR)

450 g (1 lb) shortcrust pastry

3 eggs

250 g (9 oz) ricotta cheese

50 g (2 oz) frozen peas

25 g (1 oz) chopped parsley

1/4 tspn salt or to taste

Black pepper to taste

1/2 tspn mixed dried herbs

Beaten egg for glazing

METHOD

Divide the pastry into two and roll out both pieces to fit a deep pie dish, line the pie dish with one piece and put the other piece to one side. Whisk the eggs well and then stir in the ricotta, peas, parsley, herbs, salt and pepper making sure it is well mixed. Pour the ricotta mixture into the lined pie dish and brush the edges with egg; place the remaining piece of pastry on the top trimming and pinching the edges together to seal them. Brush the top with egg and pierce the top with a fork, decorating with pastry leaves if wished. Place in a pre-heated oven at 190°C, 375°F, gas mark 5 for 30-40 minutes or until golden brown.

RED PEPPER AND GRUYERE TART

Smiles Brewery Tap is right next to the brewery in Bristol and has won a CAMRA design award. The menus are well designed, too, always offering something tempting for vegetarians, such as this savoury flan.

INGREDIENTS
(SERVES SIX-EIGHT)

Approx 750 g (1½ lbs) shortcrust pastry

750 g (1½ lbs) red peppers, sliced

2-3 cloves garlic, crushed

175 g (6 oz) grated Gruyère cheese

300 ml (½ pint) milk

1 large egg

Heaped tblspn fresh, chopped parsley

Large pinch marjoram

Black pepper

Salt

Olive oil

METHOD

Roll out pastry to line a shallow 30 cm (12") flan dish and bake blind for 15 minutes at 220°C, 425°F, gas mark 7. Saute peppers in olive oil with garlic and a good grating of black pepper until soft then spread over pastry. Cover with grated cheese. Whip milk and egg together and stir in chopped parsley and a sprinkling of black pepper. Pour over tart so the peppers are about two-thirds submerged (don't drown them). Bake at 230°C, 450°F, gas mark 8 for 20-30 minutes until tart is nicely brown on top. Serve with mixed green salad.

VEGETABLE CRUMBLE

Here is a vegetable dish from the Mad Dog, Odell in Beds, a pub brought into every edition of Good Pub Food by the cooking of Doreen Scott.

INGREDIENTS

A selection of pre-cooked vegetables (potatoes, sweetcorn, peas, tomatoes, cauliflower, courgettes, onions)
Vegetable stock
2 cloves garlic (crushed)
Crumble
225 g (8 oz) plain flour
100 g (4 oz) butter
100 g (4 oz) Cheddar
75 g (3 oz) Red Leicester

METHOD

Chop the vegetables, mix with crushed garlic then add to a vegetable sauce made with water the vegetables have cooked in and a veggie stock cube. Place in individual ovenproof dishes, or one large one, and top with a crumble mix made by rubbing flour and butter together to make crumbs, then stirring in grated Cheddar. Grate a different cheese such as Red Leicester and sprinkle over. Bake in a medium oven (190°C, 375°F, gas mark 5) for around 30 minutes and serve with minted new potatoes or salad.

CROSTINI OF MUSHROOMS AND BASIL

Here's a simple vegetarian recipe from a renowned and award-winning food pub, the Silver Plough at Pitton in Wilts.

INGREDIENTS (QUANTITIES FLEXIBLE DEPENDING ON HOW MANY YOU MAKE)

Sliced mushrooms
French baguette (preferably stale)
Good olive oil
Fresh basil
Sea salt and black pepper
Diced fresh tomato
Garlic cloves
Butter

METHOD

Cut a thick slice from the baguette; soak with olive oil and rub the surfaces with a cut garlic clove and fresh, chopped basil. When the bread is soaked, arrange all the slices you are using on a greased baking tray; top the bread thickly with sliced mushrooms, dot with butter and season well. Roast in a hot oven (230°C, 450°F, gas mark 8) for around 5 minutes until the bread is sizzling and the mushrooms cooked. Sprinkle with diced tomato and serve with a mixed salad.

CHEESY LEEK AND POTATO BAKE

From the Everyman Bistro in Liverpool, a pub which always gains Good Pub Food's "V" for excellent vegetarian food, a simple and quick meatless meal.

INGREDIENTS
(SERVES FOUR)

2 large leeks, washed and chopped

4 large, baked potatoes; cooled, peeled and sliced

250 ml (8 fl oz) double cream

250 g (8 oz) mature Cheddar, grated

Salt and pepper

Pinch of nutmeg

Pinch of snipped fresh chives

Butter

METHOD

Sweat leeks in a knob of butter until tender, add cream and season with salt, pepper and nutmeg. Layer in a gratin dish starting with leeks followed by potatoes topped with cheese, then repeat, finishing with a layer of cheese. Bake towards the top of a hot oven (220°C, 425°F, gas mark 7) until golden; garnish with chopped chives.

GARLIC POTATOES

From the Butchers Arms, Alltwen, a side dish to accompany almost any grilled steaks (vegetarian or meat).

INGREDIENTS

500 g (1 lb) potatoes, boiled

1 clove garlic

50 g (2 oz) grated Cheddar

Small carton single cream

METHOD

Slice cooked potatoes thickly and layer in a tray, sprinkling a little crushed garlic on each layer. Pour on enough cream to just reach the top layer. Top with grated Cheddar and bake in a hot oven until golden brown and bubbling.

WINTER WARMER POTATOES

Two warming winter vegetable dishes, perfect with game, or just on their own for vegetarians, from Harry Burgess, landlord/chef at the Fleece Inn, Dolphinholme, Lancs.

INGREDIENTS

Finely sliced potatoes

Thyme

Sliced onions

Salt and black pepper

Crushed garlic to taste

White wine vinegar

METHOD

Mix sliced onion, garlic, salt and pepper; place a layer of sliced potatoes into a deep, buttered ovenproof dish. Place a layer of onion mix on top, then alternate layers of sliced potatoes and onion mix ending with a layer of potatoes. Dot with large knobs of butter and a sprinkling of white wine vinegar. Cover with foil then bake in a hot oven until cooked through – 40 to 60 minutes.

SPICY RED CABBAGE

The second vegetable side dish from the Fleece Inn. Note the fairly short cooking time; all too often red cabbage is stewed to sogginess.

INGREDIENTS

1 average sized red cabbage, shredded
4 tblspns brown sugar
2 large cooking apples peeled, cored and sliced
1 wineglass red wine
1 level tblspn cinnamon
1/2 a glass red wine vinegar
1 tspn salt

METHOD

Put all ingredients in a heavy pan with a tight-fitting lid. Simmer until tender, at least 20 minutes, adding a little water if it gets too dry.

VEGETARIAN MUSHROOM CREOLE

An unusual mushroom dish from Stella Sutherland at
the Old Station Inn, Hallatrow, formerly in Avon.

INGREDIENTS
(SERVES EIGHT)

750 g (1½ lbs) button mushrooms
1 tspn mixed spice
3 medium onions, sliced
2 cloves garlic (crushed)
1 small tin pineapple chunks in juice
1 each red, green and yellow peppers, de-cored, seeded and sliced
1 tspn caster sugar
2 oz creamed coconut, grated
1 large tin chopped plum tomatoes
Black pepper and salt to taste
1 tspn fresh rosemary, chopped
3 tblspns sunflower oil
1 tspn cinnamon
1 glass red wine

METHOD

Fry onions and garlic over a low flame until soft but not coloured. Add all other ingredients except the mushrooms and diced peppers. Cook 'sauce' for about 15 minutes. Add the mushrooms and peppers and cook for a further 10 minutes; season to taste. If wished, add a little cream just before serving with boiled rice.

MUSHROOMS A LA GRECQUE

A piquant vegetarian starter comes from chef Alex de la Torre at The Anchor Inn, Oldbury-on-Severn near Bristol.

INGREDIENTS

1 onion, finely chopped
1 clove crushed garlic
150 ml (¼) pint olive oil
3 tblspns white wine vinegar
Little chopped tarragon
2 tblspns chopped parsley
Bay leaf
175 g (6 oz) button mushrooms

METHOD

Fry the finely chopped onion and the crushed garlic gently in 3 tblspns oil for 4 minutes. Add the remaining oil, wine vinegar and herbs. Simmer gently for 20 minutes. Add the whole mushrooms and simmer until just tender. Chill in the fridge overnight.

COURGETTE, MUSHROOM AND TOMATO SAUCE

From the Three Stags' Heads in Wardlow Mires, Derbyshire, a superb vegetable sauce to serve with fresh pasta.

INGREDIENTS
(PER SERVING)

1 sliced courgette

6 button mushrooms, chopped in half

Half small tin tomatoes, chopped

Knob of home-made garlic butter

4 tblspns extra virgin olive oil

1 tblspn chopped, fresh basil

Good pinch each of dried oregano and grated nutmeg

Salt and pepper

METHOD

Saute courgettes and mushrooms in garlic butter and olive oil for 2 minutes each side. Add tomatoes, oregano and nutmeg and season with salt and pepper. Lower heat, cover and simmer for 5 minutes. Add chopped basil, stir in, and serve immediately on a bed of fresh pasta – spinach tagliatelle would be particularly tasty.

GRENADINE ONIONS

This is more of a tip than a recipe and is an accompaniment to venison sausages as served at the Red Lion in Llanfihangel-Nant-Melan, Mid Wales.

INGREDIENTS

450 g (1 lb) onions, sliced

50 g (2 oz) unsalted butter

1 wineglass Grenadine

Salt and black pepper

METHOD

Gently sauté sliced onions in butter in a frying pan until translucent, but not browned. As they start to soften pour in the Grenadine and cook gently until onions are tender; season with salt and freshly ground black pepper.

ETHNIC

HOKKIEN BRAISED PORK

This delicious and colourful dish won the Guinness Pure Genius pub food awards. It comes from Soh Pek Berry, who creates stunning Malaysian and Indonesian cuisine at the Black Bull, Cliffe, Kent.

INGREDIENTS
(SERVES FOUR-SIX)

1 kg (2 lbs) leg of pork, cut into 2½ cm (1") cubes

5 tblspns light soy sauce

100 g (4 oz) Chinese mushrooms, soaked in boiling water for 30 minutes, then drained and cut into strips

3 tblspns cooking oil

5 tblspns sugar

6-8 cloves of garlic, peeled and crushed (plus 1 whole head of garlic, unpeeled, optional)

225 g (8 oz) Chinese chestnuts (available skinless in dehydrated form; soak overnight and then boil until tender)

Water

4 tblspns black soy sauce

Black pepper

METHOD

Heat oil in a heavy-based saucepan and add the crushed garlic and fry until light brown. Add pork and Chinese mushrooms and stir-fry until the meat changes colour; add both soy sauces, sugar, pepper and enough water to cover. Add whole head of garlic, if used (Soh Pek always does). Cover and simmer gently until the meat is tender and the sauce is thick, stirring occasionally; remove the head of garlic and discard; add chestnuts and simmer for a further five to 10 minutes; taste, and season with extra sugar and soy sauce to taste. It is a dish which actually improves by being prepared the day before and reheated. Serve with plain boiled rice (Soh-Pek uses long grain Phoenix rice and shapes it in a mould) and stir-fried seasonal vegetables.

MALAY CHICKEN CURRY

One of Mary Wheeler's popular S.E. Asian curries from The Horns, Crazies Hill, Berks.

INGREDIENTS

6-8 chicken pieces

1 large onion (chopped)

1 clove garlic (crushed)

Half tspn each of: turmeric powder; chilli powder; ginger powder; aniseed powder

3 cloves

4 cardamom seeds (shelled)

2 x 1 cm (½") sticks cinnamon

Juice and zest of 1 lemon and blade of lemon grass (or juice and zest of 2 lemons)

100 g (4 oz) creamed coconut

METHOD

Fry onion until soft, add garlic and spices, fry for a few minutes. Soften coconut in 300 ml (½ pint) of water and add to onions and spices. Grill the chicken pieces then pour the spare mixture over the top, cover your dish with a lid or tin foil and place in medium oven (200°C, 400°F, gas mark 6) for about 45 minutes or until cooked.

THAI PORK TENDERLOIN

Mike Maguire left an advertising career in London to be a pub chef and has won a huge reputation for the table at the Trengilly Wartha Country Inn and Restaurant near Falmouth in Cornwall. Here is one of his spicier dishes.

INGREDIENTS
(SERVES EIGHT)

225 g (8 oz) molasses

300 ml (half pint) soy sauce

100 g (4 oz) Thai red curry paste

1.5 kg (3 lbs) pork tenderloin

600 ml (1 pint) orange juice

1 carrot, chopped

2 tblspns coriander chopped

2 tblspns ginger, freshly grated

2 garlic cloves

1 large chilli, seeded and chopped

1 tblspn ground cumin

1 tblspn Thai red curry paste

METHOD

Trim the tenderloin of any fat and sinew and slice into evenly sized pieces before marinating overnight in the molasses, soy sauce and Thai red curry paste. Put all the other ingredients into a saucepan and cook gently until the carrot is tender. Whizz with a hand blender or in a processor. Pass through a fine sieve and cool; store in a jar in the fridge. Heat 1 tblspn of vegetable or groundnut oil in a heavy-based saucepan until just smoking. Add the pork and stir fry until cooked through – about five minutes, moistening with a little water as needed. Serve on a bed of noodles or rice garnished with freshly chopped coriander and with some of the hot orange sauce on the side.

STUFFED CHICKEN BREASTS THAI STYLE

Oriental chicken is bursting with fresh coriander in this main course from The Crown, Munslow, Shropshire – recipe from Vic and Stevie Pocock.

INGREDIENTS
(SERVES FOUR)

4 chicken breasts

1 small green chilli, finely chopped

1 large onion, chopped

600 ml (1 pint) chicken stock

100 g (4 oz) peeled prawns

1 dstspn Thai fish sauce

1 dstspn fresh shredded ginger

1/4 tspn Thai seven spices

1 clove garlic, crushed

2 spring onions, coarsely chopped

5 dstspns finely chopped fresh coriander (including stems and roots if possible)

1 tblspn cornflour

A little oil for frying

Juice of 1 lime

Salt and pepper

METHOD

Stuffing: sweat onion in oil without browning. Add garlic, ginger, chilli and 4 dstspns of coriander. Stir and cook gently for about 1 minute then add lime juice and prawns, mix well and season to taste. Cover and keep hot whilst preparing the chicken. Slit chicken breasts (not right through) to make envelopes. Fill each with stuffing. Close and secure with string.

To make sauce: heat chicken stock in the pan used for stuffing and stir in fish sauce, Thai seven spices, spring onions and the rest of the coriander. Place stuffed chicken breasts into the sauce mix, cover and cook on a moderate heat until chicken is tender – at least 20 minutes. When ready, lift chicken from the sauce, remove string and slice diagonally to reveal stuffing, then arrange on four heated plates. Thicken the sauce with cornflour, season and pour over the sliced breasts. Serve with soft noodles and stir-fry vegetables.

INDONESIAN FISH HOTPOT

Much of the menu at the Silver Plough at Pitton in Wilts is traditional English fare, from game to cheese, but there is an innovative side as well, such as this flavourful hotpot.

INGREDIENTS
(SERVES EIGHT)

1.5 kg (3 lbs) chunky fish fillets (eg salmon, cod)

4 tblspns oil

8 cloves garlic, crushed

2 bunches spring onions, trimmed and split lengthways

1 average jar peanut butter

2¼ litres (4 pints) chicken stock

4 fresh chillies

300 ml (½ pint) soy sauce

Pack of egg noodles

250 g (8 oz) frozen peas

METHOD

Heat oil, add spring onions and garlic, fry for 1 minute and add fish cut into fair-sized chunks. Stir in the peanut butter, chopped chillies, and soy sauce. Add stock and bring to the boil; add noodles and simmer until just cooked. Before serving add the cooked peas.

SRI LANKAN FISH CURRY

Prawn curry seems to be the scope of the fish section at many Indian restaurants but I love a real fish curry. This one comes from the spicy menu of joint cooks Michael and Deirdre Hall at the New Inn, Buckingham.

INGREDIENTS
(SERVES FOUR)

2 tblspns oil

2 tblspns finely chopped onion

2 cloves garlic, crushed

1 tblspn finely chopped ginger

1/2 tspn chilli powder

4 green chillies

300 ml (1/2 pint) diluted coconut milk

Salt

4 fish cutlets (halibut, cod, etc)

METHOD

Heat the oil in a pan, add the onion, garlic, ginger and chilli powder and fry until the onion is soft. Add the chillies, coconut milk and salt to taste and simmer until thickened. Add the fish, spooning the sauce over, and cook uncovered for about 5 minutes or until tender.

BEEF EMBUL

A second dish from the New Inn in Buckingham, where landlady Deirdre Hall cooks not only pub grub but a special Sri Lankan menu. This curry is medium hot.

INGREDIENTS (SERVES SIX)

750 g (1½ lbs) lean braising steak

1 tspn tamarind

300 ml (½ pint) water

½ tspn chilli

½ tspn white pepper

1 tspn salt

½ tspn turmeric

½ tspn lemon grass

1 stick cinnamon

Salt to taste

METHOD

Cube beef. Mix tamarind with water and remove seeds. Place tamarind water in a pan, add chilli powder, pepper, salt, turmeric, cinnamon stick and lemon grass and mix well. Add beef and simmer gently until the meat is tender and the gravy has thickened. (Add a little water during cooking if it starts to get dry). Remove cinnamon stick and serve this medium hot curry on a bed of rice with stir-fry vegetables.

SRI LANKAN OMELETTE

Deirdre Hall at the New Inn also sent this recipe for a spicy and offbeat omelette that makes a tasty supper for two.

INGREDIENTS
(MAKES 2 OMELETTES)

3 eggs
1 onion
1 green or red chilli
Sprig curry leaves
½ tspn salt
½ tspn black pepper
2 tspns cornflour
Oil for frying

METHOD

Beat the eggs. Chop the onion, chilli and curry leaves. Mix onion, chilli, curry leaves, salt, pepper and cornflour into the eggs. Heat the oil in a frying pan and when just smoking pour in half the omelette mixture. Cook for a couple of minutes, carefully turn and cook the other side. Make a second omelette with the remaining mixture.

SIAM CHICKEN

The Druid Inn at Birchover near Matlock in Derbyshire will blow your mind (or stomach) with its way-out recipes. This one, by their standards, is relatively conservative.

INGREDIENTS
(SERVES FOUR)

4 chicken joints

1 lemon (juice and zest)

½ cup Roses lime juice

2½ cm (1") fresh root ginger finely grated

1 tspn ground ginger

½ tspn salt

1 banana

1 lemon

1 lime

METHOD

Score chicken joints and place in a casserole dish; cover with all other ingredients apart from banana. Top with lid and cook in a medium oven (190°C, 375°F, gas mark 5) for approx 1 hour, until cooked. Garnish with long slices of banana and wedges of lemon and lime; serve with a crisp green salad.

NEPALESE CHICKEN KORMA

The Horns in Crazies Hill, Berks, contributed this exotic Eastern recipe for Nepalese chicken korma.

INGREDIENTS
(SERVES FOUR-SIX)

2 medium onions, finely chopped

150 ml (5 fl oz) yoghurt

Oil for frying

3 cloves garlic

2 tspns ginger, fresh or powdered

1 tspn cumin

1 tspn cardamom seeds (removed from pods)

1 tspn chilli powder

1 tspn salt

2 chicken thighs per person

METHOD

Fry chopped onion in oil until it starts to turn brown, add crushed garlic and ginger and stir, then add all the other ingredients (apart from the chicken), putting the yoghurt in last. Skin the chicken pieces and pack into a flat casserole dish. Pour the sauce over the chicken pieces, cover and cook in a pre-heated medium oven (180°C, 350°F, gas mark 4) until the chicken is tender (40-60 minutes). Serve with Basmati rice and chutney.

ALOO DUM

This recipe for Aloo Dum also came from The Horns, Crazies Hill, Berks. Try it with curry, or as a side dish with a bowl of yoghurt.

INGREDIENTS

225 g (8 oz) cooked but firm potatoes

2 tomatoes

100 g (4 oz) chopped onion

1 clove garlic (crushed)

25 g (1 oz) fresh ginger (or 1 tspn ground ginger)

15 g (½ oz) fresh coriander

2 fresh chillies (or ½ tspn chilli powder)

1 level tblspn garam masala

Salt to taste

Oil for frying

Desiccated coconut.

METHOD

Fry onion, garlic and chopped chillies or chilli powder, then add ginger and garam masala. Add diced tomatoes and cook until soft. Put in diced potatoes and cook carefully until heated through. Season with salt and turn mixture into heated dish, sprinkle with fresh coriander and desiccated coconut.

VEGETABLE CURRY

This dish from The Horns accompanies their Nepalese Chicken Curry but is also a delicious vegetarian dish on its own.

INGREDIENTS

1 medium onion, chopped
Oil for frying
1 clove garlic, finely chopped
1 tspn ginger, powdered or fresh
½ tspn chilli powder, or 2 fresh chopped chillies
½ tspn turmeric powder
1 tspn cumin powder
½ tspn coriander seed
Pinch of salt
Approx 450 g (1 lb) fresh mixed vegetables of your choice – perhaps cauliflower florets and green beans
Desiccated coconut to garnish

METHOD

Fry onion until soft; then add garlic and ginger and fry for a few seconds; then add the other flavourings and stir for a few seconds more. Add fresh vegetables and stir until coated with the mix; cover and cook very gently until just cooked, ie still slightly crunchy, and sprinkle with desiccated coconut.

MASOOR DAL WTH SLICES OF POTATOES AND NUTS

The Old Crown Inn, Hesket Newmarket, Cumbria, has a wonderful view over the countryside, a brewery at the back and an innovative menu.

INGREDIENTS
(FOR SIDE DISH)

225 g (8 oz) red lentils

50 g (2 oz) cashews

1 tspn turmeric

100 g (4 oz) sweet potatoes

225 g (8 oz) onions, half sliced, half finely chopped

2 green chillies, chopped

Quarter of a red pepper, chopped

Quarter of a green pepper, chopped

600 ml (1 pint) water

Pinch of salt

METHOD

Prepare sweet potatoes by washing, topping and tailing, then slicing into thin discs. Cook the lentils in the measured water, with salt and turmeric, removing any scum as it comes to the boil; simmer gently for around 1½ hours until tender, stirring from time to time. Fry the rest of the ingredients in a good oil; add lentils and cook together for a few minutes, stirring – the texture should be thickish but still slightly runny with the potatoes keeping their shape.

MASALA CHOPS

Michael and Deirdre Hall, licensees and joint cooks at the New Inn in Buckingham, supplied this ethnic taste.

INGREDIENTS (SERVES FOUR)

1 tspn ground cumin seeds

2 tspns ground coriander seeds

¼ tspn chilli powder

1 clove garlic, crushed

Salt

Lemon juice to mix

4 pork chops

METHOD

Mix the spices, garlic and salt to taste into a paste with lemon juice. Slash the pork chops on both sides. Rub the paste into the meat and leave for at least 30 minutes. Cook under a pre-heated moderate grill for 5 to 8 minutes on each side, depending on thickness. Serve with rice and, perhaps, a vegetable curry.

KEEMA CURRY

A tasty and inexpensive curry of minced lamb and lentils came from the Cambridge Blue in Cambridge, a pub with a snug and a Balti night.

INGREDIENTS
(SERVES FOUR)

450 g (1 lb) minced lamb
½ tspn ground cloves
1 large onion, diced
½ tspn cinnamon
100 g (4 oz) lentils
2 tspns chilli powder
2 large cloves garlic, crushed
2 tspns ginger
225 g (8 oz) mixed vegetables (optional)
2 heaped tspns cumin
Small tin tomato purée
2 heaped tspns coriander
Small tin tomatoes, chopped
2 heaped tspns turmeric
A little oil for frying
2 bay leaves
½ cup vinegar (approx)
Large pinch methi leaves

METHOD

Fry onions until soft; add crushed garlic and spices except for turmeric to produce a dryish paste. Add enough vinegar to make a moist paste and cook for up to 1 minute, until you lose the vinegar smell. Meanwhile, cook lentils separately in water to a thinnish paste. Add chopped tinned tomatoes, mince and turmeric to spices and cook for a few minutes stirring constantly; add tomato purée and mixed vegetables if desired. If it seems a bit dry, add a little water or stock. Stir in cooked lentils and simmer for 30 minutes, stirring from time to time to prevent it from sticking.

Special Brown Rice

Measure out quantity of brown rice required. Cook half of it plain in one pan; cook the other half with a pinch of rosemary, a broken stick of cinnamon, 3 chopped bay leaves and 1 tspn of turmeric. When both lots are cooked, rinse and mix together. Do not add salt during cooking.

SPICED LAMB WITH WATER CHESTNUTS

At the unusual Sun Inn, Feering in Essex, they do a fair amount of Maltese cooking, but this spicy dish has more of an oriental flavour.

INGREDIENTS
(SERVES SIX)

2.25 kg (2½ lbs) cubed lamb

1½ tblspns hoisin sauce

1 bunch chopped spring onions

1 tblspn chilli sauce

2 sticks celery

3 tspns five-spice sauce

1 courgette

2 tblspns light brown sugar

275 g (10 oz) mushrooms, sliced

150 ml (5 fl oz) red wine

3 cloves garlic, crushed

1 can water chestnuts

25 g (1 oz) fresh ginger, sliced

1 can bamboo shoots

600 ml (1 pint) chicken stock

Oil for frying

1 tblspn flour

3 tblspns light soy sauce

METHOD

Cut courgettes and celery into 3.5 cm (1½") lengths, then slice into three lengthwise. Heat oil and brown meat, then add spring onions, celery, garlic and ginger and cook until softened. Stir in flour thoroughly and cook gently for 1-2 minutes; add stock and red wine and stir until thickened before adding drained bamboo shoots, drained water chestnuts and all the other ingredients. Bring to the boil then turn down and simmer with lid on for around an hour until the meat is tender. Serve with egg fried rice.

COTES DE PORC A L'ARDENNAISE

I think David Stevenson probably serves the cheapest pub food in England – but that does not reflect its quality. At the Ship & Mitre in Liverpool you could eat this dish for £2.75 with chips and peas. I wonder if you can make it for that? Halve the ingredients for 4-5 people.

INGREDIENTS
(SERVES 10, OR GREEDY FIVE)

10 large pork loin chops, at least 2½ cm (1") thick, rind removed

450 g (1 lb) smoked ham, finely chopped

10 shallots, finely chopped

Fresh tarragon

3-4 cloves garlic, crushed

300 ml (½ pint) crème fraîche

½ bottle white wine

4-5 rounded tblspns wholegrain mustard

Plain flour

Butter for frying, preferably clarified

METHOD

Marinate the ham in the wine for at least half an hour. Lightly flour the chops before cooking slowly in butter; halfway through, add the drained ham, (reserving marinade) chopped shallots and garlic. Quickly brown everything, then deglaze with the reserved marinade. Remove the chops and keep warm. Add the crème fraîche and mustard to the sauce and reduce. Pour sauce over the chops and sprinkle over finely chopped tarragon.

CALIFORNIAN RABBIT CASSEROLE

A warming winter recipe with a bit of a twist from Lyn Coleman, joint licensee of the Scarlett Arms at Walliswood, near Ockley in Surrey.

INGREDIENTS
(SERVES EIGHT)

2 whole rabbits, jointed

4 rashers green bacon, roughly chopped

600 ml (1 pint) Californian wine

1¼ litres (2 pints) chicken stock

300 ml (½ pint) single cream

Dijon mustard

2 tspns fresh tarragon

1 tspn chives

8 shallots

Fresh parsley, chopped

METHOD

Sauté shallots, bacon and 1 tspn of tarragon in butter until shallots are translucent. Add jointed rabbit and fry quickly to seal. Add mustard, wine and stock and simmer for 30-60 minutes until the rabbit is tender. Remove from heat and stir in cream, chives and tarragon. Season to taste, sprinkle with fresh parsley, and serve.

POLLO CACCIATORA

The Tally Ho at Hatherleigh, Devon, offers a brilliant combination of home-brewed ale and cosmopolitan cuisine. Here is an recipe for Italian-style chicken in a rich tomato sauce.

INGREDIENTS
(SERVES EIGHT)

2 farm chickens

100 g (4 oz) butter

225 ml (6 fl oz) olive oil

2 large onions, finely sliced

1 kg (2 lbs) peeled tomatoes

250 ml (8 oz) chicken stock

Fresh rosemary

2 bay leaves

Salt and pepper to taste

METHOD

Clean the chickens, remove the skin and cut into medium size pieces (8-10 per chicken). Fry onions in oil and butter until golden, then remove with a slatted spoon and fry chicken pieces in same pan on all sides until golden brown. Return onions to pan with a good pinch of fresh rosemary and 2 bay leaves and stir constantly over high heat for 5 minutes. Add peeled, quartered tomatoes, turn down heat to moderate, and cook for 20 minutes. As the sauce thickens add stock to prevent it from sticking. Towards the end of the cooking time add salt and freshly ground black pepper to taste. Cook until the chicken is tender and the sauce is quite thick. Serve with new potatoes and green beans or a crisp radicchio salad.

SNACKS/
SAUCES/
PICKLES

MAD DOG CLANGER

The Mad Dog at Little Odell near Bedford is not averse to dropping the odd clanger – and here it is!

INGREDIENTS (FOR ONE)

125 g (4 oz) spicy pork sausagemeat

2 tspns sweet pickle

2 tspns cooked apple

2 tspns fried onion

2 squares of puff pastry

Beaten egg to glaze

METHOD

Place apple on a piece of pastry then the sausagemeat topped with onion and pickle. Cover with the other piece of pastry, seal into a parcel, brush with egg wash and bake for about 20 minutes at 180°C, 350°F, gas mark 4 until golden brown. Serve hot or cold.

OXFORDSHIRE BACON CLANGER

From the Dashwood Arms at Kirtlington in Oxon, a local dish to keep out the cold.

INGREDIENTS
(SERVES FOUR)

450 g (1 lb) bacon pieces

1 medium onion, chopped

1 tspn mixed herbs

Freshly ground black pepper

100 g (4 oz) shredded suet

225 g (8 oz) self-raising flour

Pinch of salt

Cold water

METHOD

Fry bacon pieces gently for 5 minutes, add chopped onion and cook for a further 2 minutes until onion is soft. Allow to cool. Make suet pastry by mixing suet, flour and salt together then adding enough water to form a dough. Roll out to an oblong approximately 1 cm (½") thick. Spread bacon mixture onto suet pastry evenly, and sprinkle with mixed herbs and a grating of black pepper. Dampen edges of pastry and roll up as if making a Swiss roll. Wrap well and neatly in greaseproof paper ensuring the whole pudding is covered; steam for about 2 hours until cooked. Slice and serve with buttered cabbage, carrots sprinkled with lemon juice and black pepper, and a rich, golden gravy, perhaps flavoured with cider.

THE DRIFTWOOD SPARS CORNISH PASTY

Jill Treleaven at the Driftwood Spars Hotel, Trevaunance Cove near St Agnes in Cornwall, says that to a Cornishman the Cornish pasty is such a sensitive subject that her recipe is bound to provoke controversy – so I salute her courage in donating it.

INGREDIENTS
(SERVES FOUR TO SIX)

450 g (1 lb) chuck steak or skirt trimmed and chopped (not minced!)

1 large onion coarsely chopped

5 medium-sized potatoes and approx half a swede, all thinly sliced not diced.

Salt and pepper.

Pastry

225 g (8 oz) plain flour

225 g (8 oz) self-raising flour

75 g (3 oz) margarine

75 g (3 oz) lard

Cold water

METHOD

Make pastry as usual, by rubbing flour and fat and adding enough cold water to bind ingredients before kneading. Keep kneading for longer than you would normally, so that when cooked the pastry is harder than usual – the original pasty was for working men to take down the tin mines or out into the fields, and there is an old saying: "You should be able to drop a good pasty down a tin mine without it breaking." Also the pastry must not be too short or the pasty will split while cooking. Divide pastry into 4 to 6 portions and roll out into circles. Mix meat with onion, potatoes and swede and season well. Divide into pastry circles, wet edges and crimp. Place on a baking sheet and bake in the centre of a pre-heated oven 190°C, 375°F, gas mark 5 for 45 to 60 minutes. Cover with foil if they start to get too brown.

SCOTCH EGGS

Hazel Milligan, once landlady at the Falklands Arms, Great Tew, one of the most beautiful villages in Britain, brought these delicious Scotch eggs to the launch of the first guide.

INGREDIENTS (MAKES 8)

1 kg (2 lbs) sausagemeat (preferably home-made)

4 tspns Worcester sauce

2 tblspns plain flour

1 tblspn sage

½ tspn paprika

Salt and pepper

8 hard-boiled eggs

1-2 beaten eggs

175 g (6 oz) fresh breadcrumbs

Oil for deep frying.

METHOD

Boil eggs the night before. Mix sausagemeat with Worcester sauce, flour, sage, paprika, pinch of salt and pepper. Mould around shelled eggs forming a 1 cm (½") layer, then brush with beaten egg and coat with fresh breadcrumbs; deep fry on medium heat in pre-heated oil for 6 minutes until golden brown. Drain on absorbent paper. Serve cold.

CULLEN SKINK

David Stirrup, a former landlord of the Lade Inn at Kilmahog, Perthshire, and his chef, Eddie Leask sent this traditional Scottish recipe – though I'd like to think there was a touch of chowder, as David hailed from Canada.

INGREDIENTS

1 onion, chopped

250 g (8 oz) potatoes, peeled and roughly chopped

500 g (1 lb) smoked haddock fillets, skinned and roughly chopped

600 ml (1 pint) fish stock

300 ml (½ pint) milk

Salt and pepper to season

Single cream to garnish

METHOD

Sauté onion and potato gently in butter without browning. Add smoked haddock and continue cooking gently for a few minutes. Add milk and simmer until the potatoes and fish are cooked through and break up to thicken the soup. Season with black pepper – you probably won't need salt because of the salty fish. Add a small quantity of single cream and bring to serving temperature without boiling. Sprinkle with fresh, chopped parsley.

GOATHLAND BROTH

The Mallyan Spout near Whitby in Yorkshire created a warming dish appropriate to the North Yorkshire Moors which can be bleak in winter, and named it after the district.

INGREDIENTS (SERVES FOUR)

500 g (1 lb) neck end lamb

50 g (2 oz) each of leeks, carrots, swede, celery, and onion, all roughly chopped

50 g (2 oz) pearl barley

1 tspn fresh, chopped rosemary

Seasoning

METHOD

Place the lamb, in pieces, in a pan with water to cover and bring slowly to a simmer. Skim well. Add all the remaining ingredients and simmer gently for 3 hours or until the meat falls from the bones. Cool rapidly by placing the pan in a sink of ice-cold water and stirring occasionally (to help prevent bacterial growth and subsequent sourness). When the broth is cold, remove bones and pick off meat. Return meat to the pan and season to taste; reheat thoroughly.

BLUE CHEESE TARTLETS

Landlord and landlady David and Janet Day cook together at the Drovers Arms, Howey, near Llandrindod Wells in Powys. Here is a truly delicious starter or veggie dish which they serve with their home-made beetroot chutney and salad.

INGREDIENTS
(MAKES EIGHT)

For herb pastry (makes approx 8 x 7.5-10 cm (3-4") tartlets)

100 g (4 oz) plain flour
100 g (4 oz) granary/brown flour
150 g (5 oz) Welsh butter
1 tspn mustard powder
1 tblspn chopped sage
1 tblspn chopped parsley
1 egg beaten with 1 tblspn water

For cheese filling

100 g (4 oz) cream cheese
100 g (4 oz) Gorgonzola
25 g (1 oz) Welsh butter
3 eggs (lightly beaten)
350 ml (12 fl oz) double cream
1½ tspns freshly ground black pepper
1 tblspn chopped chives
Salt to taste

METHOD

Make pastry in the usual way, adding the herbs and mustard to the dry flour. Wrap pastry in film and chill for 30 minutes. For filling, mix cheeses and butter, blend with cream, eggs, pepper and chives – check seasoning for salt. Roll out pastry and line tartlet tins, bake blind at 200°C, 400°F, gas mark 6 until lightly coloured then remove from oven and fill with cheese mixture. Return to oven for around 20 minutes until the filling is set and golden. Originally this recipe was made with Pencarreg blue cheese but, sadly, this is no longer made. We've successfully substituted Gorgonzola – see the photo section.

STOVIES

A favourite Scottish way of using up leftovers is a tasty dish called Stovies. Here is the version served by Tom Willis at TG's Bar at 135a George Street, Edinburgh, which sadly closed since appearing in the guide.

INGREDIENTS (SERVES SIX)

Ingredients
1kg (2lbs) potatoes
225g (8 oz) chopped roast beef or cooked sausages (or mix of both)
2 large onions
3 oz beef dripping
Water
Salt and pepper

METHOD

Peel and slice the potatoes and place in a heavy saucepan. Cover with water, season with salt and pepper, bring to the boil, then turn down and simmer for 15 minutes. Meanwhile chop the onions and lightly fry them in the dripping until clear and soft but not browned. Once the potatoes are cooked, pour off most of the water, leaving about an inch in the bottom of the pan. Return to the heat and mix in the onion in dripping and the meat. Simmer on a low heat for around 25 minutes until the liquid evaporates. Serve with Worcester sauce and cooked cabbage.

RIFT VALLEY CHICKEN LIVERS

A recipe from the Devonshire Arms, Mellor, near Stockport in Cheshire.

INGREDIENTS

225 g (8 oz) chicken livers, cut to bite-sized pieces
2 cloves garlic, finely chopped
1-2 fresh green chillies, de-seeded and finely chopped
2.5cm (1") fresh ginger, peeled and grated
1 tspn garam masala (or more to taste)
Fresh lemon juice, oil, butter, salt

METHOD

Heat a little oil and butter in a frying pan. Add garlic, ginger and chillies and stir quickly over a high heat; add chicken livers continuing to stir. Season with salt and lemon juice and when cooked quickly sprinkle with garam masala at the last moment. Serve with rice and nan or on its own, preferably with a large gin and tonic!

BACON, MUSHROOM AND CHEESE FILLED JACKETS

In some pubs they cut open jacket potatoes and pile in the stuffing. At the Chequers, Chipping Norton, Oxon, this tasty snack from Kay Reid is more satisfying.

INGREDIENTS
(SERVES FOUR)

4 large baking potatoes

100 g (4 oz) sliced mushrooms

4 rashers smoked bacon

100 g (4 oz) mature Cheddar, grated

METHOD

Bake the potatoes in the oven until soft. Grill the bacon then chop into small pieces. Saute the mushrooms in butter. Halve the potatoes and scoop out centres into a bowl; retain skins. Mix in the bacon, mushrooms and most of the cheese; season to taste. Refill potato skins carefully, sprinkle remaining cheese on top and return to a hot oven until the cheese bubbles and browns slightly. Serve with a crisp, green salad.

* I know of a pub in Somerset where the potato is scooped out and mixed with cream, cider and seasoning then reheated in the skins.

THREE ELMS CLUB SANDWICH

A classic club sandwich makes an ideal snack. Here is the popular version served at the Three Elms at North Wootton, Dorset, known for its fine sarnies and original cooking.

INGREDIENTS (PER SANDWICH)

3 slices brown bread

Mayonnaise

Carved roast chicken

Sliced ham

METHOD

Toast three slices of brown bread. Spread one slice with mayonnaise, top with chicken strips and sliced ham, spread with a little more mayonnaise and put second slice on top then repeat the process. Finish with final slice of toast, divide into quarters and skewer together with cocktail sticks. Serve with salad garnish – at the Three Elms you get chunky chips as well.

BOLOGNESE FLAN

You've heard of spaghetti bolognese. This is pastry and bolognese, from the King's Arms, Old Amersham, Bucks.

INGREDIENTS
(SERVES FOUR-SIX)

20 cm (8") short pastry case baked blind
1 sprig thyme
225 g (8 oz) best minced beef
1 bay leaf
2 cloves garlic, crushed
1/4 pint (150 ml) beefstock
100 g (4 oz) sliced mushrooms
1 tblspn tomato purée
100 g (4 oz) chopped tomatoes (can be tinned)
50 g (2 oz) chopped shallots
Salt and black pepper
15 g (1/2 oz) plain flour
Cheese sauce
25 g (1 oz) butter
300 ml (1/2 pint) milk
1 tspn French mustard
25 g (1 oz) flour
25 g (1 oz) grated, well-flavoured cheese
1 egg yolk

METHOD

Brown the meat and chopped shallots in a frying pan; add flour and rest of Bolognese ingredients and cook for a few minutes, stirring. Season to taste; pour into pastry case. For the cheese sauce, melt the butter, make a roux with the flour, add milk slowly, stirring, to make a lump-free sauce. Stir in the mustard and cheese and finally the egg yolk; remove immediately from the heat. Spoon a thin layer of cheese sauce over the top of the bolognese mixture and bake in a medium hot oven (190°C, 375°F, gas mark 5) until golden brown.

MEXICAN BURRITOS

From the Blacksmiths Arms at Preston le Skerne in Co Durham, the Cook family sent this spicy recipe for a quickly made tasty bite.

INGREDIENTS
(ONE SERVING)

2 tortillas

¼ chopped onion

¼ tspn garlic purée

¼ tspn tomato purée

¼ cup tinned chopped tomatoes

¼ chopped chilli

¼ cup pinto beans (canned, drained and rinsed)

¼ cup Gouda, grated

Half tblspn olive oil

Crème fraîche

¼ tblspn chopped coriander

Salsa

METHOD

Fry onion and chilli in oil until onions soften. Add garlic and beans, crushing them slightly whilst frying. Add tomato purée and chopped tomatoes in juice (not too wet), then coriander and stir for a few minutes. Warm tortillas and spread mixture on them, sprinkle with grated cheese, roll up and serve with a garnish of chopped coriander, crème fraîche and salsa.

PEACH, ONION AND RED PEPPER RELISH

Just delicious with pork chops, fried chicken and cold gammon is this pithy pickle from Lynn Lowes of the Black Lion at Butterton in Staffs.

INGREDIENTS
(SERVES SIX)

6 medium peaches, de-stoned and sliced, or equivalent canned peaches

2 tblspns lemon juice

1½ cups chopped red pepper

1¼ cups chopped onion

2 tblspns curry powder

½ tspn cayenne pepper

½ cup firmly packed golden brown sugar

½ cup cider vinegar

Salt and pepper

½ cup coriander leaves

METHOD

Chop peach slices into smaller pieces and combine with lemon juice. Place red pepper and onion in a little oil in a saucepan then sweat over low heat until vegetables are tender, but still crisp – about six minutes. Add curry powder and cayenne pepper, and stir for about a minute. Add sugar, and stir until dissolved, then cider vinegar and stir for another 2 minutes. Add peach mixture and cook until heated through – around 3 minutes. Season to taste and mix in coriander leaves. Cool and store in covered container in fridge.

APPLE CHUTNEY

Heather Humphreys is a cracking cook normally famed for her amazing home-made pies. At the Rising Sun, Woodland, near Ashburton in Devon she even makes the chutney herself.

INGREDIENTS

1.5 kg (3 lbs) bramley apples
1.5 kg (3 lbs) onions
300ml (½ pint) water
450 g (1 lb) sultanas or raisins
750 g (1½ lbs) demerara sugar
600 ml (1 pint) malt vinegar
2 tspns ginger
¼ tspn cayenne pepper
5 whole peppercorns
4 cloves
1 tspn ground mace
½ tspn nutmeg
Rind and juice of 2 lemons

METHOD

Chop the onion finely. Peel and chop the apple. Cook the onion in 300 ml (½ pint) water for 10 minutes. Add the apple, sultanas or raisins, lemon rind and juice, demerara sugar and spices and simmer until tender. Add the vinegar and simmer until it reaches a thick jam consistency. Pour into clean dry warm jars and seal at once.

BAY HORSE APRICOT AND APPLE CHUTNEY

Bob Lyons, former head chef of the Miller House at Windermere, makes a fabulous chutney which I have enjoyed with air-dried Cumbrian ham, while gazing over Morecambe Bay from the Bay Horse at Ulverston, Cumbria.

INGREDIENTS

225g (½ lb) dried apricots

600 ml (1 pint) malt vinegar

225g (½ lb) bramley apples, peeled, chopped and sliced

1 tspn ground ginger

75g (3 oz) allspice berries

450 g (1 lb) onions, quartered

450 g (1 lb) brown sugar

50g (2 oz) sea salt

METHOD

Put onions and apples through the mincer to create moisture before putting apricots through. Bring to simmering point one third of the vinegar and add to this the salt and ginger plus allspice in a muslin bag. Then add the apricot, apple and onion mix. Simmer over a low heat until thick. Meanwhile, dissolve the sugar in the remaining vinegar and then add to the thickened mixture in the pan. Simmer again without a lid until thick; leave to cool, then pot and seal.

TANGY BARBECUE SAUCE

Here is the recipe for Tangy Barbecue Sauce which has accompanied dishes at the Fox & Hounds in Skeffington, Leicester.

INGREDIENTS

1 small onion

1 small green pepper

2 tspns cooking oil

6 tblspns good quality tomato ketchup

3 tblspns white wine vinegar

3 tblspns demerara sugar; 1 tblspn Worcester sauce

1 tspn English mustard

METHOD

Finely chop onion and green pepper and cook slowly in the oil until both are soft. Mix remaining ingredients together and add to the hot mixture. Cook slowly, stirring continuously for a further 10 minutes until the sugar is dissolved. Excellent with burgers and barbecues.

PUDDINGS

STEAMED MARMALADE CASTLES

Here is another delicious, sweet-toothed recipe from passionate cook Kim Scicluna of the Sun Inn at Feering in Essex.

INGREDIENTS
(SERVES FOUR TO SIX)

4-6 tblspns orange marmalade

1 tblspn whisky

100 g (4 oz) unsalted butter

100 g (4 oz) caster sugar

2 eggs plus 1 egg yolk, beaten

225 g (8 oz) self-raising flour

To serve:

Sprigs of mint and grated nutmeg

Custard

Orange rind

METHOD

Lightly grease 4-6 individual moulds or a 900 ml (1½ pint) ovenproof basin. Mix the whisky and marmalade together and spoon evenly into the bases of the moulds or basin. Cream the butter and sugar together until pale and fluffy, then beat in the eggs, including the extra yolk. Fold in the flour with a metal spoon until evenly combined. Divide the mixture evenly between the moulds or fill the basin and cover with a piece of pleated foil. Steam the small puddings for about 40-50 minutes or the large one for 1½ hours, or until well risen. Serve with custard mixed with a little orange rind. Decorate with sprigs of mint and a little grated nutmeg and serve immediately.

MISS LILY'S ECCLEFECHAN TART

A proper pudding contributed by 18th century Creebridge House Hotel, Newton Stewart in Dumfries, former home of the Earl of Galloway.

INGREDIENTS
(SERVES FOUR)

Pastry base:

375g (12 oz) plain flour
175g (6 oz) butter
2 eggs

Ecclefechan filling:

450g (1 lb) sultanas
125g (4 oz) butter
125g (4 oz) demerara sugar
1 dstspn white vinegar
4 eggs, beaten

METHOD

Pastry base
Rub flour and butter together to make fine crumbs; beat eggs and add to mix to form a stiff dough. Roll out and line 23cm (9") flan dish.

Filling
Melt butter and mix with other ingredients to form sloppy mix. Pour into pastry case and bake in pre-heated oven – 190°C, 375°F, gas mark 5 – for around 40 minutes until set and golden brown.

OLD ENGLISH TREACLE TART

This recipe from the Royal Oak at Lostwithiel, Cornwall, is an interesting old-fashioned version of treacle tart incorporating apple.

INGREDIENTS
(SERVES SIX)

28cm (11") shortcrust pastry case, part baked blind.

425 ml (15 fl oz) golden syrup

50 g (2 oz) fresh breadcrumbs

½ tspn powdered ginger

Grated zest and juice of half a lemon

Grated zest and juice of half an orange

2 tblspns soft brown sugar

2 tblspns thick cream

1 apple, peeled, cored and grated

1 tspn butter

Beaten egg to glaze

METHOD

Melt the syrup in a saucepan, stir in the breadcrumbs, ginger, grated zest and juice of orange and lemon, soft brown sugar, thick cream, grated apple and butter. Blend well and pour into the half-baked pastry case. Roll out leftover pastry trimmings and cut into strips; use to cover tart weaving over and under to create lattice effect. Brush lattice with beaten egg yolk; bake in moderately hot oven (200°C, 400°F, gas mark 6) for around 25 minutes or until golden brown. Allow to cool before serving with clotted cream.

CHOCOLATE BREAD AND BUTTER PUDDING

Alison Clark at the Miners Arms, Nenthead in Cumbria, regularly updates a cookbook of the recipes enjoyed by diners at the pub. Here is a variation on a very old pub standard.

INGREDIENTS
(SERVES FOUR-SIX)

10 slices buttered bread
600 ml (1 pint) skimmed milk
175g (6 oz) plain chocolate
50g (2 oz) sugar
1 splash vanilla essence
1 tspn cinnamon
2 eggs
50g (2 oz) crushed hazelnuts

METHOD

Heat the milk to boiling point, add the sugar, vanilla essence, cinnamon and chocolate, stirring until the chocolate has melted, then leave to cool. Beat the eggs in a bowl, then gradually add the chocolate milk, stirring all the time. Line a greased baking dish with bread and sprinkle some of the nuts evenly over the top; continue layering the bread and nuts until both have been used up, ending with a layer of bread. Pour the chocolate mixture over the bread and nut layers and cook in a medium oven – 190°C, 375°F, gas mark 5 – for 45 minutes to 1 hour. Serve with chocolate custard or whipped cream.

SPICY HOSTRY BREAD PUDDING

Pauline Parker is still performing culinary feats at The Hostry Inn, Llantilio Crossenny, Monmouthshire in Wales.

INGREDIENTS

225 g (8 oz) stale wholemeal bread
300 ml (½ pint) milk
225 g (8 oz) sultanas
50 g (2 oz) glacé cherries
50 g (2 oz) soft margarine
100 g (4 oz) soft brown sugar
1 tblspn ground mixed spice
1 large egg
Fresh ground nutmeg (plenty to put on top!)

METHOD

Break up the bread and put into the mixing bowl with the milk. Leave to soak. Add the fruit, margarine, sugar and spice. Beat well. Whisk the egg and add to the mixture. Put in a shallow buttered ovenproof dish, press down and sprinkle well with nutmeg. Bake in the oven at 180°C, 350°F, gas mark 4, for about 45 minutes. Can be eaten hot or cold, served with custard, cream or ice cream.

BREAD AND BUTTER PUDDING

Puddings are scrummy at the Crown, Elsenham, on the Essex/Herts border. There are some irresistible home-made ice creams such as marmalade with gin, but here is a rich and unusual version of a classic pud.

INGREDIENTS
(SERVES 8-10)

1 litre (1¾) pints *whipping cream*

125 g (4 oz) *sugar*

4 egg yolks

75g (3 oz) *sultanas*

3 tblspns *sherry*

6-8 slices *buttered bread, crusts removed*

Apricot jam

METHOD

Whisk egg yolks and sugar until thick and pale. Heat cream until almost boiling and pour onto the egg mixture; stir in sherry and leave to stand for 5 minutes. Cut bread into triangles and arrange in a 1.75 litre (3-pint) shallow dish with sultanas scattered between slices; pour liquid over bread and leave to stand for 15 minutes while bread soaks it up. Place in bain marie in a medium oven at 190°C, 375°F, gas mark 5, until custard has set. To brown top, place under hot grill for 20 seconds. Melt some apricot jam and brush over the top; delicious hot or cold.

APPLE CHARLOTTE MALTESE STYLE

A second dessert from the Sun Inn, Feering in Essex, where you often find a Maltese flavour through the antecedents of landlord Charlie Scicluna. Dishes of his homeland have been recreated by his English wife, Kim.

INGREDIENTS
(SERVES SIX)

1 kg (2 lbs) cooking apples, peeled, cored and sliced

2 tblspns dark rum

100 g (4 oz) brown sugar

150 ml (¼ pint) white wine

25 g (1 oz) butter

Rind of 1 lemon, grated

Slices of bread and butter with crusts removed

METHOD

Put the apples in a pan with the sugar, wine and lemon rind and cook until tender. When the fruit is reduced to a pulp add the butter and extra sugar if wished. Grease a soufflé dish and line it with the buttered bread, pour in the fruit pulp, and over the top place another layer of buttered bread. Sprinkle with a little brown sugar and bake in a moderate oven (190°C, 375°F, gas mark 5) for 30 minutes or until golden. Just before serving pour over the rum and serve with pouring cream or ice cream.

HOT OAT AND BANANA SLICE

This short, sweet recipe comes from the Maypole Inn at Long Preston near Skipton in North Yorkshire.

INGREDIENTS

100 g (4 oz) butter
100 g (4 oz) soft brown sugar
100 g (4 oz) rolled oats
2 eggs (beaten)
4 ripe bananas

METHOD

Melt the butter and sugar over a gentle heat. Add the oats and eggs. Put half the mixture in tray, cover with sliced bananas and then the rest of the mixture. Bake in moderate oven (180°C, 350°F, gas mark 4) for 30-45 minutes, until golden brown. Serve with thick yellow cream.

GLAZED STRAWBERRIES IN HORSERADISH AND BLACK PEPPER SABAYON

Here is a wonderfully unusual and sophisticated way to dress up strawberries, sent from the White Hart, Great Saling, in Essex, by Nicholas Knight.

INGREDIENTS

2 egg yolks

1 cup double cream

Caster sugar

A pinch cracked black peppercorns

Small pinch fresh grated horseradish

1 punnet strawberries

Vanilla ice cream

Demerara sugar

METHOD

To make the sabayon, whisk yolks and cream over boiling water, add caster sugar to taste. When at ribbon stage, add black pepper and horseradish to taste (horseradish should be just a hint on the palate). Place a scoop of vanilla ice cream in an individual deep dish. Top with strawberries then coat with sabayon. Sprinkle with a little demerara sugar and serve immediately.

INDIVIDUAL VICTORIAN TRIFLE WITH STRAWBERRIES

From the Olde White Horse in Midhurst, West Sussex, came a wonderfully rich and indulgent – not to mention alcoholic – old–fashioned trifle.

INGREDIENTS

6 macaroons

Egg custard

600 ml (1 pint) single cream

2 egg yolks

2 eggs

1 tblspn cornflour

Caster sugar to taste

Madeira and brandy

Strawberries

Ratafia biscuits

Topping

300 ml (½ pint) double cream

50 g (2 oz) sugar

125g (4 oz) white wine or sherry

2 tblspns brandy

Pared rind and juice of 1 lemon

Extra double cream for piped rosettes

METHOD

Cut macaroons to fit six individual dessert trifle dishes; moisten with Madeira and brandy. Prepare egg custard by whisking eggs and yolks, cornflour and sugar together; warm cream gently and pour onto egg mixture, then heat very gently in a thick pan stirring all the time, until the mixture thickens; cool slightly and spoon over macaroons and leave to set. Arrange halved strawberries over custard once firm. Mix white wine, brandy and lemon and leave to stand for at least an hour, then strain. Add sugar and stir until dissolved; add cream and whisk gently until it holds its shape. Spoon over strawberries. Decorate with ratafia biscuits, strawberry halves and cream rosettes.

NEGRONI ALLA PANNA

The Anchor Inn, South Somercotes, Lincs, featured in the second guide with lovely Italian dishes. Landlady Maria Nicholson sent me three recipes, and I chose this rich, alcoholic dessert.

INGREDIENTS
(SERVES FOUR-SIX)

3 small cartons *whipping cream*

½ *measure Campari*

½ *measure Martini Rosso*

1 *measure vodka*

1 *tblspn cranberry sauce*

Sugar to taste

'Cigarette' biscuits

METHOD

Whip two cartons of cream until it starts to stiffen; add the other ingredients and fold in well. Three-quarters fill tall goblets with the mixture; top with remaining cream,whipped stiffly and sweetened with sugar. Place a 'cigarette' biscuit in each goblet.

ORANGE AND BRANDY SYLLABUB

Old-fashioned syllabub from Christine and Martin Baucutt of the Shepherds Inn, Melmerby, Cumbria, a multi–award winning pub for its food.

INGREDIENTS
(SERVES 10-12)

600 ml (1 pint) double cream
175 ml (6 fl oz) cream sherry
1 measure brandy
1 measure concentrated orange juice
75 g (3 oz) caster sugar
Finely grated rind and juice of 1 large orange
1 orange for decoration

METHOD

Place sherry, brandy, concentrated orange and the rind and juice of 1 orange with the sugar in a mixing bowl. Quickly stir together, then add the double cream. Whip slowly until stiff and spoon into sundae glasses. Decorate each with twist of sliced orange. Refrigerate until ready to serve.

WHITE CHOCOLATE AND BAILEY'S MOUSSE

The Anchor Inn at Beer in Devon is well known for seafood. But here's a dessert from chef Neil Harding that has nothing to do with fish – or even with beer. . .

INGREDIENTS

225g (8 oz) white chocolate

1 tblspn Bailey's liqueur

2 tspns instant coffee

3 sheets leaf gelatine

600 ml (1 pint) double cream

2 egg whites, stiffly beaten

Plain dark chocolate for decoration

METHOD

Melt the white chocolate in a bain marie (or in a dish over a pan of just bubbling water). Mix the coffee powder with a little hot water. Put three quarters of cream into a thick bottomed pan, add the coffee and Bailey's; heat gently but do not boil. Soak the gelatine in cold water. When the chocolate has melted put it into a large mixing bowl, add the warm cream mixture and beat until smooth. Drain the gelatine and mix it in. Put the mixture in a cool place or refrigerate, stirring regularly until it reaches the ribbon stage. Fold in the stiffly beaten egg whites. Put the mixture into individual dishes then refrigerate for at least 2 hours. Decorate with a swirl of cream and a sprinkling of grated dark chocolate.

SUMMER FRUIT SURPRISE

Doreen Scott at the Bell, Odell, in Bedfordshire not only took her rural hostelry into every edition of the guide – she donated a recipe for every guide as well.

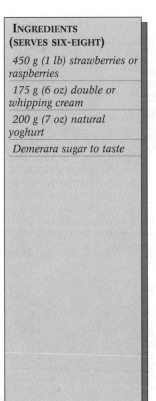

**INGREDIENTS
(SERVES SIX-EIGHT)**

450 g (1 lb) strawberries or raspberries

175 g (6 oz) double or whipping cream

200 g (7 oz) natural yoghurt

Demerara sugar to taste

METHOD

Put fruit in large bowl, or divide between wine glasses to two-thirds full. Slightly whip cream and mix in yoghurt. Spoon onto fruit and allow to run through by tapping gently on the table. Top with a thick layer of Demerara sugar and chill for 36-48 hours.

CARAMELISED TART LEMON TART

Here's a tartly lemony tart from Jean Thaxter, landlady of The Angel at Burford, Oxon.

INGREDIENTS

Shortcrust pastry to line flan dish
6 lemons
300 g (9 oz) sugar
6 eggs, beaten
Caster sugar

METHOD

Line flan dish with rolled out shortcrust pastry, bake blind till crisp (around 15-20 minutes) and allow to cool. Take zest and juice from six lemons, add the sugar and beaten eggs, then put in a glass bowl and place over a pan of simmering water, stirring until very thick. Pour into the pastry case, smooth the top and sprinkle with a little caster sugar; place under a pre-heated very hot grill until caramelised. Serve cold with thick, yellow cream.

DIXIE BOURBON PIE

A last "after" thought from the Shepherds Inn, Melmerby, Cumbria, and more exciting interpretation of the usual Banoffi pie.

INGREDIENTS (SERVES 10)

Base

375 g (12 oz) digestive biscuits, crushed

125g (4 oz) melted butter

25 g (1 oz) grated chocolate

Filling

175 g (6 oz) evaporated milk

30 marshmallows

300 ml (½ pint) double cream, whipped

1½ measures Bourbon

Grated chocolate to decorate.

METHOD

Mix crushed biscuits, melted butter and grated chocolate then mould into a 25cm (10") dish with a removable base. Place evaporated milk and marshmallows in a pan; heat gently, stirring constantly, until marshmallows melt; do not allow to boil. Cool by placing pan in cold water; then add two-thirds of whipped cream and Bourbon; stir well. Pour onto base and refrigerate. When set, decorate with remainder of double cream and grated chocolate.

DICTIONARY OF BEER

This newly compiled dictionary contains the words listed below and thousands of other definitions and descriptions to make it a unique specialist dictionary. The book will be a useful purchase for individuals, institutions and businesses with an involvement in the drinks industry – employing millions, all with training needs. Not to mention those who are interested in beer as a hobby or leisure interest.

Dictionary of Beer
by CAMRA
256 pages   Price: £7.99
Use the following code to order this book from your bookshop: ISBN 1-85249-158-2

CAMRA the Campaign for Real Ale began in 1971 as a reaction against bland keg beers foisted on the public by the national brewers...
Cask condition the quintessence of Real Ale. The beer put into the cask must contain enough yeast for a slow secondary fermentation to take place. This fermentation produces the subtle matured flavours that distinguish Real Ale from dead keg beers.
Children's certificates for some time these have been operating in Scotland, England and Wales. Licensees have to apply to their local licensing authority to be granted a children's certificate...
Christmas Ales rich festive ales, often available in polypins, are brewed by a number of British brewers...

BEER
RECIPES

CHEESE AND ALE SOUP

Hazel Milligan, for a long time landlady at the Falkland Arms at Great Tew in Oxon, sent me this simple yet extremely tasty (and filling) recipe for Cheese and Ale Soup.

INGREDIENTS

25g (1 oz) butter
1 large onion
1 slightly heaped tblspn plain flour
300 ml (½ pint) ale
300 ml (½ pint) stock
300 ml (½ pint) milk
225 g (1 lb) Cheddar
1 tspn English mustard
Salt and pepper
Pinch of mixed herbs

METHOD

Slice onions and sauté in butter until soft; stir in flour, then stir in beer, stock and milk and add the mustard, seasoning and herbs. Bring to the boil then simmer, stirring, until thickened; remove from heat and add cheese chopped in small pieces; stir gently over a low heat until it is smooth.

BROCCOLI AND STILTON SOUP

Giving a bit of hop bite to the start of the meal is Beverley Stanyer, landlady at the Railway Ale House at Stockport in Greater Manchester.

INGREDIENTS
(SERVES SIX)

2 heads of broccoli

600 ml (1 pint) pale hoppy beer (I use Hop Back Summer Lightning)

600 ml (1 pint) water

1 vegetable stock cube

1 knob butter/margarine

175 g (6 oz) strong ripe Stilton

Salt and pepper to taste

METHOD

Chop the broccoli into small florets. Melt the butter in a large, heavy based saucepan. Add the broccoli and toss to coat in the butter, then pour in the beer, cover with a tight-fitting lid and steam gently for 10 minutes. Add water and stock cube and simmer for a further 10 minutes. Mash or purée the soup. Season to taste. To serve: place 25 g (1 oz) crumbled Stilton in bowl and ladle soup over. Serve immediately with hot, crusty bread.

WELSH RAREBIT WITH ABBOT ALE

Cheese and beer really are made for each other, so here is another recipe from an enthusiastic real ale cook, Doreen Scott at the Bell in Odell, Beds.

INGREDIENTS

65g (2½ oz) butter

65g (2½ oz) plain flour

450 ml (¾) pint milk

100 g (4 oz) grated Cheddar cheese

½ tspn cayenne pepper

½ tspn mustard powder

½ tblspn Worcester sauce

1 egg yolk

150 ml (¼ pint) Abbot Ale

METHOD

Melt the butter in a saucepan, gradually add the flour, mix and cook for a few minutes. Gradually add the milk and mix to a thick, smooth sauce. Simmer, stirring, for a few minutes. Add the grated cheese and allow to melt over a low heat. Add the cayenne pepper, mustard powder and Worcester sauce; stir well. In a separate small saucepan boil the Abbot Ale until it has reduced to about a tablespoonful, then add it to the cheese sauce and stir it in. Allow it to cool and thicken before using. Spread thickly on buttered toast and brown under a hot grill. Comments Doreen: "Of course you can use any beer for the rarebit but it goes without saying Abbot Ale's the best!"

Cheese and Ale Soup
Home-made soup, smooth and satisfying, from Hazel Milligan at the Falkland Arms at Great Tewin in Oxfordshire.

Blue Cheese Tartlets
Landlord and landlady David and Janet Day cook together at the Drovers Arms, Howey, near Llandrindod Wells in Powys. Here is a truly delicious starter or veggie dish which they serve with their home-made beetroot chutney and salad.

Make the herb pastry with a mixture of plain flour and granary/brown flour, plus Welsh butter, mustard powder, chopped sage and chopped parsley and an egg with water. Create the cheese filling from cream cheese, blue cheese (we used Gorgonzola but you could use a local blue of your own choice), Welsh butter, 3 eggs (lightly beaten), double cream, freshly ground black pepper, chopped chives and with salt to taste.

Make the pastry, adding the herbs and mustard to the dry flour. Wrap the pastry in film and chill for 30 minutes. For the filling, mix cheeses and butter, blend with cream, eggs, pepper and chives – check seasoning for salt. Roll out the pastry and line the tartlet tins. Bake blind at 200 C, 400 F, gas 6 until lightly coloured, then remove from oven and fill with cheese mixture. Return to oven for around 20 minutes until the filling is set and golden.

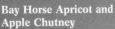

Bay Horse Apricot and Apple Chutney

Chutneys, pickles and snacks are unique to pub cuisine and there's a whole section devoted to them in this book. This chutney contains dried apricots, malt vinegar, Bramley apples, ground ginger, all-spice berries, onions, brown sugar and sea salt.

White Horse Somerset Pork

A rich regional meat dish using cider as a marinade. Pork and onions are marinaded in cider and water for 1 hour before simmering in milk.

White Horse Somerset Pork
This is the invention of Anne
Williamson at the White Horse Inn
at Stogumber in Somerset. Serve
with potatoes and vegetables.

Summer Fruit Surprise
A delicious fruity finish from
Doreen Scott at the Bell in Odell,
Bedfordshire.

ALE FONDUE

Don't give the Swiss all their own way with the fondue. Create a thoroughly English version using a pint of bitter and chunk of Cheddar.

INGREDIENTS
(SERVES FOUR PEOPLE)

600 ml (1 pint) strong flavoured bitter

450 g (1 lb)Cheddar, chopped small

1 small onion, finely chopped

1 crushed clove of garlic

1 tspn finely chopped fresh coriander

1 tspn dry mustard

Black pepper.

METHOD

Sweat onion and garlic in butter then add beer and heat; add cheese and cook gently until it has melted (if it doesn't seem thick enough add a little cornflour mixed with milk). Add the dry mustard and fresh coriander and stir well; season with plenty of freshly ground black pepper. As a dip use fresh-baked, crusty, mixed-grain bread.

WINGS OF SKATE

Beer comes into its own when making batters of all kinds. It is especially good in a fish batter, used here by The Crown at Melton Mowbray for coating wings of skate before frying.

INGREDIENTS
(TO COAT 12 PIECES)

100 g (4 oz) flour

Salt and pepper

1 tblspn olive oil

200 ml (7 fl oz) beer

2 egg whites

A little fresh dill.

METHOD

Sift the flour into a bowl and season with salt and pepper; make a well in the centre of the flour. Add the oil and gradually whisk in the beer, working from the centre outwards. Whisk only for as long as it takes to produce a smooth batter, do not overwork the mixture. Leave the batter to rest for about an hour at room temperature, otherwise it will shrink away from the fish pieces and provide an uneven coating. Add the fresh dill and beat the egg whites until they form soft peaks and fold them gently into the batter mixture just before using. Deep fry 3-4 pieces at a time in good oil, keeping them warm until all are cooked.

COD IN BEER BATTER

As I said before, beer is brilliant in any batter, from pancakes to Yorkshire pudding. Here Michael Collis, head chef at the Swan Hotel in Arundel, West Sussex shows how to use it in a really crisp, light coating batter.

INGREDIENTS
(SERVES EIGHT)

8 cod fillets

300 ml (½ pint) Arundel Best Bitter

150 ml (¼ pint) soda water

350 g (12 oz) plain flour

1 tblspn freshly chopped mixed herbs

2 tblspns malt vinegar

1 tspn ground turmeric

Pinch of salt and pepper

METHOD

Place the flour, mixed herbs, salt, pepper and ground turmeric in a bowl and mix. Add malt vinegar, soda water and ale and whisk until a smooth batter is achieved. Flour cod fillets, coat in batter and deep fry in medium hot oil until golden brown. (For best results use fresh clean oil.)
Drain on kitchen paper and serve with real chips and mushy peas.

FISHERMAN'S PIE

Here is an old favourite pepped up with a drop of bitter by Dawn Saunders of the Rose and Crown at Oundle in Northants, proving that beer really does go with fish.

INGREDIENTS
(SERVES EIGHT)

1.25 kg (2½ lbs) large potatoes

450 g (1 lb) smoked fish skinned and diced into 1 cm (½") pieces

450 g (1 lb) white fish skinned and diced into 1 cm (½") pieces

225 g (8 oz) cooked Atlantic prawns

100 g (4 oz) butter

150 ml (¼ pint) Mansfield Riding Bitter (or a good quality real ale)

3 sprigs fresh parsley finely chopped

900 ml (1½ pints) béchamel sauce

150 ml (¼ pint) double cream

METHOD

Put Riding Bitter and 25 g (1 oz) butter into pan. Heat until butter has melted, add the smoked and white fish, cover and steam until just tender, add prawns, 85 ml (3 fl oz) double cream, chopped parsley and béchamel sauce and cook on a low heat for 20 minutes. Peel, boil and mash the potatoes. Add rest of butter and cream and, using hand blender, cream until all lumps are removed. Three-quarter fill a large ovenproof dish with the cooked fish mixture, top with the creamed potato, mark with a fork, bake in a medium oven until the potato is crisp topped and golden brown. Serve with fresh green vegetables.

WELLINGTON GREENE

Recipes are often inspired by tastes from the past. The Olde White Horse near Midhurst, West Sussex, has served a 14th-century recipe for hare marinated in ale, as well as pike with brandy and Madeira. This one is reminiscent of the richly spiced dishes of the Elizabethan manor house kitchen.

INGREDIENTS
(SERVES SIX)

750 g (1½ lbs) flaky pastry

6 tblspns lamb stock

6 x 75g (3 oz) lamb noisettes

1½ tblspns Abbot Ale

275g (9 oz) crabmeat

Beaten egg to glaze

4½ tspns spice mix of coriander, turmeric, cumin

Sauce

6 tblspns lamb stock

2 tblspns Abbot Ale

½ tspn ginger, cinnamon, and chilli or a good quality mild curry powder

METHOD

Boil together for 30 seconds 4½ tspns spice mix, stock and ale, then mix into the crabmeat. Fry lamb noisettes in butter briefly (should still be pink in the centre); cool. Roll out pastry and divide into six pieces placing a noisette in the centre of each, with a dollop of the crabmeat mix on top. Gather pastry around noisette to cover and brush with egg; decorate with pastry leaves. Stand in a cool place for 30 minutes then bake in a hot oven (220°C, 425°F, gas mark 7) for 30 minutes until crisp and golden. Mix the sauce ingredients and heat, stirring.

BELHAVEN RABBIT

Named after the brewery producing St Andrew's Ale, this rabbit cooked in beer is the dish from the Boathouse, South Harbour Street in Ayr.

INGREDIENTS
(SERVES SIX)

1 rabbit, approx 1.5-1.75kg (3-4 lb)
2 cloves garlic, roughly chopped
50g (2 oz) diced carrot
1 bay leaf
50g (2 oz) diced celeriac
Zest from 2 pieces of orange peel
50g (2 oz) diced celery
1 tspn honey
50g (2 oz) diced turnip
75g (3 oz) diced cold butter
1¼ litres (2 pints) St Andrew's Ale
85 ml (3 fl oz) concentrated meat stock
2 sprigs fresh thyme
1 tblspn double cream

METHOD

Joint rabbit and marinate in beer, thyme, garlic, bay leaf and orange zest for 24 hours. Remove rabbit pieces from marinade, pat dry and fry quickly on all sides to brown and seal, then place in an ovenproof dish. Pour marinade into the pan used for frying the rabbit and simmer briskly with honey and stock until reduced by half. Add the vegetables to the rabbit and strain the reduced beer stock over, then cover with foil and bake in the centre of a medium oven (180°C, 350°F, gas mark 4) until the rabbit is tender, around 1-1½ hours depending on tenderness of the rabbit. Remove rabbit from the stock and keep warm. Reduce stock again, whisking in the butter to make it glossy, then finish by stirring in the cream. Place the rabbit on a plate coated with the sauce and serve with boiled rice and green vegetables.

LAMB PIE WITH APRICOTS AND OLD SPECKLED HEN

The Rising Sun at Woodland in Devon, is famous for its strong, country cooking and especially pies. In this one, landlady Heather Humphreys uses Morland Old Speckled Hen – even though it's not a poultry pie!

INGREDIENTS

Flaky pastry

350g (12 oz) strong, plain flour

100 g (4 oz) margarine

100 g (4 oz) lard and around 225 ml (⅓ pint) of water (or 750 g (1½ lb) shortcrust or frozen puff)

1 onion, chopped

1 tspn ginger

tblspn chopped fresh mint

600 ml (1 pint) Old Speckled Hen

1.5kg (3 lbs) leg of lamb (boned and cubed)

Stock (made from bones) and seasoning

175g (6 oz) dried apricots, chopped

Cornflour

METHOD

Put all the ingredients apart from the pastry into a saucepan, add the Old Speckled Hen and enough stock to cover. Season with salt and pepper. Bring to the boil and simmer gently for an hour or 90 minutes until tender; allow to cool, then skim off any fat, reheat and thicken with 2-3 tblspns cornflour dissolved in cold water; simmer rapidly for 2-3 minutes to thicken pie filling. Check seasoning and leave to cool. Roll out pastry and line pie dish or flan tin. Tip in meat mix and top with the remaining pastry, using trimmings to make a hen to decorate. Bake in a pre-heated oven at 200°C, 400°F, gas mark 6, for 25 minutes until the pastry is golden brown.

BRAISED BEEF WITH MURPHY'S AND KUMQUATS

Beef in ale is a bit of a cliché, but this recipe from the Ivy House at Chalfont in Bucks gives it a twist by using stout with orange juice and kumquats.

INGREDIENTS
(SERVES SIX)

1.25 kg (2½ lbs) braising beef

2 large onions (diced)

600 ml (1 pint) Murphy's or other stout

300 ml (½ pint) beef stock

150 ml (¼ pint) orange juice

10 kumquats sliced into rings

METHOD

Fry the onions until golden. Add the braising beef and brown lightly. Add Murphy's and beef stock and simmer for approximately two hours, until the beef is tender. Add the orange juice and the kumquats. Season to taste and thicken with a little cornflour. Serve with a few kumquat rings on top for decoration.

STEAK AND STILTON PIE

Barbara Wood serves all sorts of delicious traditional dishes at The Three Cups Inn, Punnets Town, Heathfield in East Sussex. Here is her recipe for a hearty steak, Stilton and ale pie.

INGREDIENTS
(SERVES SIX)

1.25 kg (2½ lbs) chuck steak
1 large onion, chopped
600 ml (1 pint) Harveys (or any real ale)
300ml (½ pint) beef stock
1 tblspn gravy granules
450 g (1 lb) shortcrust pastry
175 g (6 oz) Stilton (approx)

METHOD

Fry onion until soft, add steak and fry until browned, then add ale and stock and simmer gently until cooked (about two hours), adding water if necessary, then gravy granules to thicken and season. When the meat is tender, transfer into a large pie dish, roll out the pastry and place on pie, seal and glaze with beaten egg and cook at 200°C, 400°F, gas mark 6 for approx 30 minutes until brown.

VENISON COLLOPS WITH CRANBERRIES AND SHALLOTS SERVED WITH DEEP FRIED CELERIAC

Game is at its best with ale, as in this supper party dish from Alistair Horn, head chef of the Boot Inn, Boothsdale in Cheshire.

INGREDIENTS
(SERVES FOUR)

4 venison steaks

350 g (12 oz) peeled shallots

1 small head of celeriac (peeled and cut into thin strips)

1 punnet cranberries (or 2 tblspns of cranberry sauce)

150 ml (¼ pint) Old Ale

Salt and pepper

A little sugar

METHOD

Seal the venison in an oiled frying pan, add the shallots and roast in the oven for 10 minutes. Remove the pan from the oven. Remove the venison and keep warm. Add the cranberries and the beer and boil until reduced by half. (Sugar can be added if the cranberries are very sour.) Thicken the sauce by whisking in small cubes of butter. Arrange venison steaks on four plates, pour round the gravy and serve with deep fried celeriac.

HIGHGATE STEAK PUDDING

Highgate Mild is one of my favourite beers to cook with, adding a dark spiciness. This recipe from the Swan Inn, Pelsall, in the West Midlands is irresistible in a giant Yorky.

INGREDIENTS
(SERVES SIX)

1.25 kg (2½ lbs) diced stewing steak

50 ml (2 fl oz) vinegar

1 tspn mixed herbs

1 bay leaf

900 ml (1½ pints) Highgate Mild

Tin of tomatoes

Gravy browning

175 g (6 oz) field mushrooms, sliced

Six large Yorkshire puds, preferably home-made with ale in!

METHOD

Place steak, vinegar, herbs and bay leaves in a large saucepan and marinate for 30 minutes. Completely cover with water and bring to the boil, add half the Highgate Mild and tomatoes. Cook for 1½ hours, then add the rest of the beer. Add mushrooms and thicken with gravy granules. Cook for another 45 minutes and serve up in giant Yorkshire Puddings, with vegetables and jacket potatoes.

BRAISED BEEF WITH BROWN ALE AND WILD MUSHROOMS

The Old Hall Inn at Threshfield, North Yorks has been in every issue of Good Pub Food for its splendid ever-changing menus. Wild mushrooms and Newcastle Brown bring a new depth to this recipe for braised beef.

INGREDIENTS (SERVES SIX)

1 kg (2 lbs) best braising steak (cut into 100g (4 oz) pieces)

100 g (4 oz) mixed wild mushrooms

2 diced onions

4 cloves garlic

Fresh thyme

1 bottle Newcastle Brown Ale

600 ml (1 pint) beef stock

50 g (2 oz) sugar

2 bouquet garnis

METHOD

Seal braising steak on both sides in a hot pan, set aside in an ovenproof casserole dish, deglaze the pan with the ale and reduce by about half. Meanwhile fry the onions, thyme, garlic and sugar until golden brown. Add the wild mushrooms, fry for 2 minutes and then add the reduced brown ale and the stock and reduce by a third. Pour the liquid into the casserole with the beef, add the bouquet garni and cook with the lid on in a moderate oven, 180°C, 350°F gas 4 for approximately 2 hours, thicken sauce with cornflour and season to taste.

HOME-MADE SAUSAGES

It's worth finding the time to make your own sausages because they taste so good. Here Ian Dutton, of the Dutton Arms at Burton on the Cumbria border, flavours them with just a little beer.

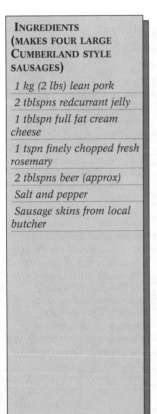

INGREDIENTS
(MAKES FOUR LARGE
CUMBERLAND STYLE
SAUSAGES)

1 kg (2 lbs) lean pork

2 tblspns redcurrant jelly

1 tblspn full fat cream cheese

1 tspn finely chopped fresh rosemary

2 tblspns beer (approx)

Salt and pepper

Sausage skins from local butcher

METHOD
Mince pork (ask butcher, but better to do it yourself to ensure pork is lean). In a bowl mix minced pork, redcurrant jelly, cream cheese, rosemary and beer to a stodgy mixture. Fill skins with sausage skin device or piping bag. Seal in a frying pan then bake in oven. Serve as a main meal with traditional mash and onion gravy.

HAGGIS, POTATO AND TURNIP FRITTERS SERVED WITH A REAL ALE AND ONION GRAVY

It's great to take a traditional dish and reinvent it, as in this recipe from the Nether Abbey Hotel at North Berwick in Scotland.

INGREDIENTS
(SERVES FOUR TO SIX)

Ingredients
225 g (8 oz) haggis
225 g (8 oz) potatoes
225 g (8 oz) turnip
225 g (8 oz) onions
450 ml (¾ pint) demi-glacé (stock)
150 ml (¼ pint) real ale
Plain flour
1 egg, beaten with a little milk
Seasoning
Breadcrumbs
Parsley to garnish

METHOD

Peel, chop and boil potatoes until cooked. Peel, chop and boil turnips until cooked. Drain the potatoes and turnips, place in a bowl with the haggis and mash together, add salt and pepper to taste. Peel and slice the onions, place in a pan with a little oil and cook for 3-4 minutes. Add the demi-glacé and real ale, season and continue to cook for a further 5 minutes. Roll the haggis mixture into small balls, roll in flour followed by egg wash and then into the breadcrumbs. Deep fry the haggis fritters in hot oil for 3 minutes. To serve – place some real ale and onion gravy on a plate, enough to cover the base. Place two to three fritters in the centre of the plate and garnish with a sprig of parsley. Serve with mustard mash.

PUMPKIN, APPLE AND BEER CHUTNEY

Sparkling dishes are the order of the day from Mary Wilson, licensee of O'Hara's at Forfar in Scotland. Here is her gorgeous recipe using ale as a preservative in a chutney that would be perfect with Ian's sausages. She brought a jar all the way from Scotland for the launch of the fifth Good Pub Food Guide!

INGREDIENTS

1 large onion, chopped

275 g (10 oz) diced pumpkin

4 diced and peeled cooking apples or windfalls

15 g (½ oz) fresh ginger grated

50 g (2 oz) brown sugar

600 ml (1 pint) ale – dark and strong (Orkney Dark Island for preference)

½ tspn turmeric powder

½ tspn crushed garlic

Salt

METHOD

Put all ingredients into a large pan and bring to boil; simmer until cooked through. Mash roughly leaving some chunky bits. Cover and cool, then put in jars and seal well. Great as part of a Ploughman's or with the beer sausages.

BEER CHEESE

Here's a delicious way to partner cheese 'n' ale from Karen Mounsey, chef and landlady at the Aldchlappie Hotel, Kirkmichael in Tayside, Scotland.

INGREDIENTS
(SERVES 15-20)

1 kg (2 lbs) sharp Cheddar at room temperature

2 cloves garlic, mashed

3 tblspns Worcestershire sauce

2 tspn dry mustard

Tabasco to taste

Half bottle Scottish beer, approx

1 tspn salt, to taste

METHOD

Cut the cheese into cubes and place them in a food processor or electric mixer. Process until perfectly smooth. Add the garlic, Worcestershire sauce, mustard and tabasco. Blend well. Add the beer, a little at a time, while continuing to beat the cheese, until the mixture is a good, firm spreading consistency. (Too much beer will make the cheese too fluffy.) Stir in the salt, and refrigerate. (This keeps superbly.) Serve on small slices of rye or pumpernickel bread. Delicious with cold, cold beer.

BEER TART

And beer is still there for the sweet course as Kim Scicluna, imaginative chef at the Sun Inn, Feering, Essex, shows with this very moreish tart.

INGREDIENTS

115 g (4½ oz) butter

200 g (7 oz) plain flour sifted

1 tblspn castor sugar

Pinch of salt

200 ml (7 fl oz) strong beer

2-3 tblspns iced water

200 g (7 oz) soft brown sugar

2 large eggs

METHOD

Rub 90 g (3½ oz) of the butter into the flour with the sugar and salt. Mix in enough water to bind the dough together and chill for 30 minutes. Heat oven to 200°C, 425°F, gas mark 7. Roll out pastry and line 23 cm (9") tart tin. Sprinkle the brown sugar over the pastry base. Break the eggs in a bowl and beat in the beer. Pour through a sieve directly onto the sugar, then cut the remaining butter into slivers and scatter over the tart. Cook for 30 minutes until the filling is just firm to touch. Leave to stand for at least 10 minutes before serving warm, or allow to cool before serving with cream.

CAMRA'S GOOD CIDER GUIDE

CAMRA's guide to real cider researched anew for the new
Millennium and now with features on cider around the world
– North America, France, Spain.

The guide contains three main sections:

Features on cider-making from around the world, bottled
cider and cider traditions.

⇔ A comprehensive and detailed guide to UK producers of
cider. Each producer entry includes details of the ciders
produced, availability, cost, and visitor information. There
are also notes on the producer's cider-making background
and history. All this data is newly surveyed by the editor and
a huge team of CAMRA volunteers.

⇔ A brand new listing of outlets – pubs, restaurants, bars,
small cider makers – with full address including postcode
and telephone contact numbers. Details of ciders available
and, where appropriate, items of interest in the pub or area.

CAMRA's Good Cider Guide
by David Matthews
256 pages   Price: £9.99
Use the following code to order this book from your
bookshop: ISBN 1-85249-143-4

CIDER

RABBIT WITH CIDER AND CORIANDER

The sweetness of cider and fresh coriander combine with rabbit in a casserole from the Old Black Lion at Hay-on-Wye, Hereford.

INGREDIENTS
(SERVES FOUR)

2 medium rabbits

300 ml (½ pint) chicken stock

1 medium onion, chopped

2 tspns chopped coriander

2 rashers of bacon, chopped

Sprig of thyme

2 bay leaves

175g (6 oz) mushrooms, sliced

Seasoning

600 ml (1 pint) cider

Beurre manié to thicken

METHOD

Cut rabbits into front legs, back legs and 3-4 sections from the saddle. Seal in hot oil in a casserole until brown on both sides, then remove from pan. Add onion, bacon and mushrooms and sauté until soft. Return rabbit to pan, add herbs and seasoning, cover with cider and bring to the boil. Thicken with the beurre manié and bake in a moderate oven until the rabbit is tender, around 90 minutes. Serve with croutons.

SAUSAGE CASSEROLE

I discovered the Fat Cat, Llandudno, while celebrating my wedding anniversary at CAMRA's 1997 AGM, and am grateful to Paul Evans for sending this filling dish. He made it using award-winning herby sausages from Edwards of Conwy.

INGREDIENTS
(SERVES FOUR)

8 prime pork and herb sausages
2 tblspns mustard
8 rashers middle bacon
4 medium onions, chopped
1 litre (1 ¾ pints) stock
600 ml (1 pint) cider
2 tblspns tomato purée
Seasoning
Mixed herbs
2 tspns sugar

METHOD

Brown sausages, smother with mustard and wrap with bacon. Place in suitable ovenproof dish, cover with chopped onions, mix together all other ingredients and pour over sausages; cover with foil and casserole for 1½ hours at 180°C, 350°F, gas mark 4. Drain off liquid and reduce until thickened. Adjust seasoning if needed and pour back over sausages. Best served on a bed of garlic mashed potato.

PORC MYNWY CYLCHIAN Ô GIG PORC MEWN DDWR Ô SATS A WINWNS

A Welsh dish created at the Punch House in Monmouth, Gwent with the name translated into Welsh by a friend of the proprietor. **Monnow Pork Medallions of pork in sage and cider gravy**.

INGREDIENTS

Diced lean pork (cubed) approx 225 g (8 oz) per portion

Pork bone, rind, trotter etc (for stock)

Your choice of amounts of:

onions; leeks; potatoes; cooking apples; sage; cider

Lard or rendered home-cured bacon

Plain flour

Mustard; salt; black pepper

METHOD

Remove green leek tops, shred and place in saucepan with pork bone etc. Cover with water and boil to extract maximum flavour; strain. On cooling the liquid should jelly. Peel and core apples and chop with potatoes and onions in a vertical cutter, or grate them. Add to strained liquid and boil; add cider. Toss cubed pork in a mix of sage with mustard and seasoning. Fry pork in lard, strain excess fat and essence back into frying pan. Add pork to the contents of saucepan, stew until meat is tender but not disintegrating. Return frying pan to stove and with a wooden spoon stir in flour until all fat is taken up. Gradually add liquid to the pan stirring and tasting all the time. Add extra sage and seasoning to taste. Take an old tablespoon (which should be kept for this purpose), part fill with sugar, hold with a gloved hand over gas flame until black and bubbling, plunge spoon into contents of frying pan, stir vigorously until the contents take on a nuance. Return contents of frying pan to saucepan containing pork and considerably reduce liquid. Serve with white bulb ends of leeks, boiled potatoes and vegetables in season.

STUFFED TURNIPS BAKED IN CIDER

Nicola Harris produces some lovely vegetarian dishes at the New Barrack Tavern in Sheffield and has contributed a really unusual one to the most recent *Good Pub Food* guide.

INGREDIENTS
(SERVES SIX)

6 baby turnips
125 g (4½ oz) ground hazelnuts
250 g (9 oz) field mushrooms
3 cloves garlic, crushed
1 tblspn soy sauce
Butter
Pepper
300 ml (½ pint) cider
2 bay leaves
Pinch thyme
1 tblspn ground rice

METHOD

Peel turnips then take a slice off the bottom so they stand flat, using an apple corer to hollow out the centres. Place in a buttered ovenproof dish. Finely chop the mushrooms and fry gently in butter until soft and starting to release juices. Add soy sauce and crushed garlic and set aside. In another pan toast hazelnuts (without oil) until starting to brown. Empty into a food processor and grind to breadcrumb consistency; add mushroom mixture and blast again. Stuff this mixture into turnips, and place them in an ovenproof dish, pouring in enough cider to reach halfway up turnips; add bay leaves and thyme. Cover with foil and cook at 230°C, 450°F, gas mark 8 until tender (about 1 hour). When cooked, pour liquid into small pan, mix 1 tblspn ground rice with a little water, add to pan, bring to the boil stirring all the time, then serve with the turnips. Baked cabbage and mashed potatoes go particularly well with this dish.

CIDER PIE

Here is an unusual dessert recipe from the cookbook of the Sun Inn, Feering in Essex, recipes collected and used in the pub by licensees Charlie and Kim Scicluna.

INGREDIENTS

175 g (6 oz) plain flour

¼ tspn salt

2 tspns sugar

100 g (4 oz) cold butter

50 ml (2 fl oz) iced water

Filling

15 g (½ oz) butter

235 ml (8 fl oz) maple syrup

50 ml (2 fl oz) water

600 ml (1 pint) strong cider

2 eggs, separated

1 tspn grated nutmeg

METHOD

Make the pastry by rubbing the butter into the flour and salt until it resembles breadcrumbs; add iced water and combine together with a fork to make a dough. Place in a sealed bag and chill for at least 20 minutes. Meanwhile, place the cider in a saucepan and boil until only 175 ml (6 fl oz) remains, then cool. Roll out the pastry and line a 23 cm (9") pie dish; chill for 20 minutes. To make the filling, place the butter, maple syrup, water and reduced cider in a pan and simmer gently for 5-6 minutes. Remove the pan from the heat and leave the mixture to cool slightly, then whisk in the beaten egg yolks. Whisk the egg whites in a large bowl until they form stiff peaks. Add the cider mixture and gently fold until evenly blended. Pour the mixture into the prepared pastry case, dust with nutmeg and bake for 30-35 minutes or until the filling is well set and golden brown. Serve warm.

CAMRA BOOKS

The CAMRA Books range of guides helps you search out the best in beer (and cider) and brew it at home too!

Buying in the UK

All our books are available through bookshops in the UK. If you can't find a book, simply order it from your bookshop using the ISBN number, title and author details given below. CAMRA members should refer to their regular monthly newspaper What's Brewing for the latest details and member special offers. CAMRA books are also available by mail-order (postage free) from: CAMRA Books, 230 Hatfield Road, St Albans, Herts, AL1 4LW. Cheques made payable to CAMRA Ltd. Telephone your credit card order on 01727 867201.

Buying outside the UK

CAMRA books are also sold in many book and beer outlets in the USA and other English-speaking countries. If you have trouble locating a particular book, use the details below to order with your credit card (or US$ cheque) by mail, email or fax (+44 1727 867670).

Carriage of £3.00 per book (Europe) and £6.00 per book (US, Australia, New Zealand and other overseas) is charged.

UK Booksellers

Call CAMRA Books for distribution details and book list. CAMRA Books are listed on all major CD-ROM book lists and on our Internet site: http://www.camra.org.uk

Overseas Booksellers

Call or fax CAMRA Books for details of local distributors. Distributors are required for some English language territories. Rights enquiries (for non-English language editions) should be addressed to the managing editor.

CAMRA GUIDES

Painstakingly researched and checked, these guides are the leaders in their field, bringing you to the door of pubs which serve real ale and more…

Room at the Inn 2nd edition

by Jill Adam

324 pages   Price: £8.99

This second edition of the hugely popular Room at the Inn is your guide to quality overnight accommodation with a decent selection of real ale for good measure. The guide has been completely resurveyed and researched from scratch by the grass roots experts of the Campaign for Real Ale. Each entry in the guide gives local directions, contact details, opening times, type and extent of accommodation, list of beers, meal types and times, easy to understand price guide and snippets about local attractions and the sometimes centuries-old tales associated with your resting place. Use the following code to order this book from your bookshop: ISBN 1-85249-150-7

Heritage Pubs of Great Britain

by Mark Bolton and James Belsey

144 pages hard back   Price: £16.99

It is still possible to enjoy real ale in sight of great craftsmanship and skill. What finer legacy for today's drinkers? Feast your eyes and toast the architects and builders from times past. This full colour collectible is a photographic record of some of the finest pub interiors in Britain. Many of the pubs included have been chosen from CAMRA's national inventory of pub interiors which should be saved at all costs. As a collector's item. As such it is presented on heavy, gloss-art paper in a sleeved hard back format. The pub interiors have been photographed by architectural specialist Mark Bolton and described in words by pub expert James Belsey.

Available only from CAMRA – call 01727 867201 (overseas +44 1727 867201)

Pubs for Families

by David Perrott

308 pages   Price: £8.99

Traditional pubs with CAMRA-approved ale and a warm welcome for the kids! Nothing could be better. But where to find such a hospitable hostel on home patch, let alone when out and about or on holiday? Invaluable national coverage with easy to use symbols so that you know what facilities are available and regional maps so you'll know how to get there. Get the best of both worlds. Use the following code to order this book from your bookshop: ISBN 1-85249-141-8

Good Pub Food 5th edition

by Susan Nowak

448 pages approx   Price: £9.99

The pubs in these pages serve food as original and exciting as anything available in far more expensive restaurants. And, as well as the exotic and unusual, you will find landlords and landladies serving simple, nourishing pub fare such as a genuine ploughman's lunch or a steak and kidney pudding. Award-winning food and beer writer Susan Nowak, who has travelled the country to complete this fifth edition of the guide, says that 'eating out' started in British inns and taverns and this guide is a contribution to an appreciation of all that is best in British food…and real cask conditioned ale.

Use the following code to order this book from your bookshop: ISBN 1-85249-151-5

50 Great Pub Crawls
by Barrie Pepper
256 pages   Price: £9.99

Visit the beer trails of the UK, from town centre walks, to hikes and bikes and a crawl on a train on which the pubs are even situated on your side of the track!

Barrie Pepper, with contributions and recommendations from CAMRA branches, has compiled a 'must do' list of pub crawls, with easy to use colour maps to guide you, notes on architecture, history and brewing tradition to entertain you.

Use the following code to order this book from your bookshop: ISBN 1-85249-142-6

GOOD BEER GUIDES

These are comprehensive guides researched by professional beer writers and CAMRA enthusiasts. Use these guides to find the best beer on your travels or to plan your itinerary for the finest drinking. Travel and accommodation information, plus maps, help you on your way and there's plenty to read about the history of brewing, the beer styles and the local cuisine to back up the entries for bars and beverages.

Good Beer Guide to Belgium, Holland and Luxembourg
by Tim Webb
286 pages   Price: £9.99

Discover the stunning range and variety of beers available in the Low Countries, our even nearer neighbours via Le Tunnel. Channel-hopping Tim Webb's latest edition – the third – of the guide offers even more bars in which an incredible array of beers can be enjoyed. There are maps, tasting notes, beer style guide and a beers index to complete the most comprehensive companion to drinking with your

Belgian and Dutch hosts.

Use the following code to order this book from your
bookshop: ISBN 1-85249-139-6

Good Beer Guide to Northern France

by Arthur Taylor

256 pages   Price: £7.99

Discover the excitement of the bars and cafes, the tranquillity
of the village breweries which hold the secrets of generations
of traditional brewing. Join the many festivals and cultural
events such as the beer-refreshed second-hand market in
Lille and the presentation of the Christmas ales. Find out
where the best beer meets the best mussels and chips. Cuisine
à la bière and more! Arthur Taylor is a leading authority on
French beer and a member of Les Amis de la Bière, who have
co-operated in the research for this book.

Use the following code to order this book from your
bookshop: ISBN 1-85249-140-X

Good Bottled Beer Guide

by Jeff Evans

128 pages   Price: £9.99

When early nights and unfriendly traffic conspire to keep you
at home, there's no risk these days of missing out on drinking
a fine real ale. Britain's off-licences and supermarkets now
stock bottle-conditioned ales – real ale in a bottle. The book
describes the ingredients and history behind Britain's
traditional bottled beer, and conjures up the tastes and
smells.

Use the following code to order this book from your
bookshop: ISBN 1-85249-157-4

Good Beer Guide

edited by Roger Protz

500 pages approx   Price: £11.99

Produced annually in early October

Fancy a pint? Let CAMRA's Good Beer Guide lead the way.
Revised each year to include around 5,000 great pubs serving
excellent ale – country pubs, town pubs and pubs by the sea.
Fully and freshly researched by members of the Campaign for
Real Ale, real enthusiasts who use the pubs week in, week
out. No payment is ever taken for inclusion. The guide has
location maps for each county and you can read full details

of all Britain's breweries (big and small) and the ales they produce, including tasting notes.

CAMRA's Good Beer Guide is still Britain's best value pub guide – a must for anyone who loves beer and pubs.

Cellarmanship

by Ivor Clissold

144 pages   Price: £6.99

This book explains every aspect of running a good cellar and serving a great pint of real ale which does both pub and brewer proud. It's a must have book for all professionals in the drinks trade, for all those studying at college to join it, and for all those who need to tap a cask of real ale for a party or beer festival.

Use the following code to order this book from your bookshop: ISBN 1-85249-126-4

BREW YOUR OWN

Learn the basics of brewing real ales at home from the experts. And then move on to more ambitious recipes which imitate well-loved ales from the UK and Europe.

Brew your own Real Ale at Home

by Graham Wheeler and Roger Protz

194 pages   Price: £8.99

This book contains recipes which allow you to replicate some famous cask-conditioned beers at home or to customise brews to your own particular taste.Conversion details are given so that the measurements can be used world-wide.

Use the following code to order this book from your bookshop: ISBN 1-85249-138-8

Brew Classic European Beers at Home

by Graham Wheeler and Roger Protz

196 pages   Price: £8.99

Keen home brewers can now recreate some of the world's classic beers. In your own home you can brew superb pale ales, milds, porters, stouts, Pilsners, Alt, Kolsch, Trappist, wheat beers, sour beers, even the astonishing fruit lambics of Belgium... and many more. Measurements are given in UK, US and European units, emphasising the truly international scope of the beer styles within.

Use the following code to order this book from your bookshop: ISBN 1-85249-117-5

Home Brewing

by Graham Wheeler

240 pages   Price: £8.99

Recently redesigned to make it even easier to use, this is the classic first book for all home-brewers. While being truly comprehensive, Home Brewing also manages to be a practical guide which can be followed step by step as you try your first brews. Plenty of recipes for beginners and hints and tips from the world's most revered home brewer.

Use the following code to order this book from your bookshop: ISBN 1-85249-137-X

OTHER BOOKS

CAMRA Quiz Book

by Jeff Evans

128 pages   Price: £3.99

Fun and games for beer fans, and their relations. Use this book to quiz your mates on real ale and CAMRA history. Great for fund-raising quiz events and for catching up on the campaign.

Use the following code to order this book from your bookshop: ISBN 1-85249-127-2

Kegbuster Cartoon Book

by Bill Tidy

72 pages, including colour cartoons   Price: £4.99

A classic, hilarious, collection of cartoons from well-known funny man and cartoonist extraordinaire Bill Tidy. The perfect gift for the beer lover in your life!

Use the following code to order this book from your bookshop: ISBN 1-1-85249-134-5

Brewery Breaks

by Ted Bruning

64 pages   Price: £3.99

A handy pocket guide to brewery visitor centres and museums. Keep this in the car on your travels and you'll never be far from the living history of brewing. An ideal reference for CAMRA members, and others, wishing to organise a trip to one of Britain's best known breweries or a tasting at a local microbrewery.

Use the following code to order this book from your bookshop: ISBN 1-1-85249-132-9

JOIN CAMRA

If you like good beer and good pubs you could be helping to fight to preserve, protect and promote them. CAMRA was set up in the early seventies to fight against the mass destruction of a part of Britain's heritage.

CAMRA wants to see genuine free competition in the brewing industry, fair prices, and, above all, a top quality product brewed by local breweries in accordance with local tastes, and served in pubs that maintain the best features of a tradition that goes back centuries.

As a CAMRA member you will be able to enjoy generous discounts on CAMRA products and receive the highly rated monthly newspaper What's Brewing. You will be given the CAMRA members' handbook and be able to join in local social events and brewery trips.

To join, complete the form below and, if you wish, arrange for direct debit payments by filling in the form overleaf and returning it to CAMRA. To pay by credit card, contact the membership secretary on (01727) 867201.

I/We wish to join the Campaign for Real Ale and agree to abide by the Rules.

Name(s) ....

Address ....

....

Postcode ....

Signature ....

Date ....

I/We enclose the remittance for:

Single:	£14	Joint	£17 (at same address)
OAP Single	£8	OAP Joint	£11 (at same address)
Unemployed/Disabled	£8		
Under 26	£8	date of birth:	

For Life and Overseas rates please contact CAMRA HQ
(tel: 01727 867201

Send your remittance (payable to CAMRA) to:
The Membership Secretary, CAMRA, 230 Hatfield Road, St Albans, Herts., AL1 4LW

Instruction to your Bank or Building Society to pay by Direct Debit

Please fill in the whole form using a ball point pen and send it to:

Campaign for Real Ale Ltd,
230 Hatfield Road,
St. Albans,
Herts
AL1 4LW

Originator's Identification Number

| 9 | 2 | 6 | 1 | 2 | 9 |

Reference Number

| | | | | | | | | | | | | | | | | | |

Name of Account Holder(s)

— — — — — — —

Bank/Building Society account number

| | | | | | | | |

Branch Sort Code

| | | | | | |

Name and full postal address of your Bank or Building Society

To The Manager   Bank/Building Society

Address

Postcode

FOR CAMRA OFFICIAL USE ONLY
This is not part of the instruction to your Bank or Building Society

Membership Number

Name

Postcode

Instructions to your Bank or Building Society
Please pay CAMRA Direct Debits from the account detailed on this instruction subject to the safeguards assured by the Direct Debit Guarantee. I understand that this instruction may remain with CAMRA and, if so, will be passed electronically to my Bank/Building Society

Signature(s)

Date

Banks and Building Societies may not accept Direct Debit instructions for some types of account

✂ -

This guarantee should be detached and retained by the Payer.

The Direct Debit Guarantee

■ This Guarantee is offered by all Banks and Building Societies that take part in the Direct Debit Scheme. The efficiency and security of the Scheme is monitored and protected by your own Bank or Building Society.

■ If the amounts to be paid or the payment dates change CAMRA will notify you 10 working days in advance of your account being debited or as otherwise agreed.

■ If an error is made by CAMRA or your Bank or Building Society, you are guaranteed a full and immediate refund from your branch of the amount paid.

■ You can cancel a Direct Debit at any time by writing to your Bank or Building Society. Please also send a copy of your letter to us.